Stotty 'n' Spice Cake.

The Story of North East Cooking

compiled by Bill Griffiths

This is the first volume of three resulting from the dialect project 'Wor Language', supported
by the Heritage Lottery Fund. For more information go to www.worlanguage.co.uk

Published by Northumbria University Press
Trinity Building, Newcastle upon Tyne NE1 8ST, UK

First Edition Published 2006
Second Edition Published 2006

British Library Cataloguing in Publication Data. A Catalogue Record for this book is available from the British Library.

ISBN-10: 1–904794–21–1

ISBN-13: 978–1–904794–21–9

Designed and printed by University Graphics, Northumbria University.

Typeset in Garamond

Northumbria University is the trading name of the
University of Northumbria at Newcastle. 188952

Permissions

We gratefully acknowledge the permission of the British Library to quote from MSS *Lansdowne 1033* and *Egerton 2868*.

Bell/White MS 12 – by permission of the Special Collections and Archives Librarian, Robinson Library Special Collections, University of Newcastle.

Michael Dodd's List of Geordie Words – at Beamish North of England Open Air Museum's Regional Resources Centre; and quotations from transcripts.

Rev. J.E. Hull – *A popular introduction to the Tyneside Dialect* (typescript in the Archives of the Natural History Society of Northumbria (Hancock Museum)).

Quotations from:

http://members.tripod.com/~aofieFinn/oven.html by permission of Aoife Finn (Lisbeth Herr-Gelatt).

http://www.terrycummins.clara.net/pic/kites.htm by permission of Terry Cummins.

Memories of a Geordie by Tom Moreland.

and *Teisdal' and how 'tis spokken* by Kathleen Teward.

And thanks to…

The staff at Beamish Museum's Regional Studies Centre, in particular Rosie Alan and Jo Bath; and the staff of Newcastle Central Library's Local Studies department for their generous co-operation.

Also:

Alison Bond, Jean Crocker, Jim Cromarty, George Darby, Peter Elliott, Fred Stainthorpe, Les Gorse, Jack Gair, Don Gray, Joe Henry, Eveline Johnson, Eleanor King, Bill Lancaster, Florie Merihein, Dave Neville, Ronald Orange, Joyce Oxley, Gordon and Edith Patrickson, Harry Peart, Joan Taylor Phillips, Margaret Reed, Vivian Ripley, Fred Stainthorpe, Meg and William Stephenson, Mrs E. Stirling, John Thompson, Charles Trelogan, Norman Wilson, Vic Wood… and the many others, who have participated and assisted in this project.

A special thanks to Tom Richardson, for the illustrations.

Thanks to Mara Helen Wood at the Northumbria University Gallery for the cover illustration by Norman Cornish.

Photographs by Jimmy Forsythe, courtesy of Tyne & Wear Archive Service.

Bill Griffiths is project co-ordinator for the new dialect initiative 'Wor Language', based at the Centre for Northern Studies, Northumbria University. With partners Beamish Open Air Museum and the Durham & Tyneside Dialect Group, and support from the Heritage Lottery Fund, the aim is to explore and explain North East dialect in subject groups, drawing together the responses of people from all over the region and their interpretations of dialect words relating to everyday life and work.

Stotty 'n' Spice Cake is the first book in the 'Wor Language' trilogy. If you like this book you may also be interested in:

Pitmatic: The Talk of the North East Coalfield (2007) and **Fishing and Folk: Life and Dialect on the North Sea Coast** (2008) – both by Bill Griffiths..

Comment and participation welcome.

Of interest: www.worlanguage.co.uk

CONTENTS

Setting the table

Cooking is a topic that relates not only to woman and home but holds a respectful interest for all of us that eat. It also serves as a fascinating window on North East history, society and dialect – and that is the viewpoint of the following study, that brings together public responses at dialect meetings, from correspondence, questionnaires and printed sources from all over the region.

There are two main themes – the story of cooking on an open fire and that of cooking with kitchen range and the oven – with recipes included in their appropriate place. There is only a brief look at the world of post-oven cooking. A glossary section lists and analyses the dialect words involved, under subject headings and a final part (it may be the best) contains longer examples of dialect writing, past and present.

Please note that the recipes – sensible though they seem – have not been tested by us and should be regarded as guides. Exact recipes are always to be treated with some caution – they seldom suit every cooker or every cook and there will be many workable local variants for each recipe. Improvisation, adaptation and sheer trial and error are essential skills in the kitchen, as you will learn (if you have not already done so).

With thanks to the Heritage Lottery Fund, main partners and many individual enthusiasts, 'Wor Language' is proud to present this first fruit of the new dialect project, in the belief there is plenty of useful information here, and (hopefully) some fun too.

If there are things we have missed, or could do better, let us know, and future editions will benefit from your kind assistance.

Bill Griffiths

Weights and measures

25g	1 oz
50g	2 oz
75g	3 oz
100g	5 oz or $^1/_4$ lb
225g	8 oz or $^1/_2$ lb
450g	16 oz or 1 lb
1kg	2.2 lb

30ml	1 fluid oz
60ml	2 fl.oz
90ml	3 fl.oz
150ml	5 fl.oz or $^1/_4$ pint
300ml	10 fl.oz or $^1/_2$ pint
450ml	15 fl.oz or $^3/_4$ pint
600ml	20 fl.oz or 1 pint

Abbreviations:

tisp – teaspoon

dessert spn – dessertspoon

tabspn – tablespoon

pt – pint

oz – ounce

lb – pound (weight)

'Stewart Beveridge's birthday party' by Jimmy Forsythe (1957).

Tyne & Wear Archive Service, P.4/29.

Part one – the open fire

Noo give me a weel banked fire an' a kettle on the hob – that's what ah call comfort.

(Scott Dobson in *Stotty Cake Row*, 1971)

The wood fire

The hearth was the focal centre for the house and whether that was walled with sticks and daub or local stone and roofed with straw, heather or rough limestone slabs, there are two generalities we can assert of the medieval homestead:

1. The fire would be in the middle of the floor of the main room (often the only room).

2. The typical fuel would be wood – not precluding the use of dried cow-dung ('cassons'), heather, furze ('whinns, for baking' are mentioned in the expenses of Sherburn Hospital, 1686) or peat.

The hearth would be a circle of beaten earth, probably ringed with stones. A grate to lift the fire up is not strictly needed. Nonetheless, in smarter households, the placing and arranging of new logs could be managed with the help of a set of firedogs. These took the form of an iron stand that provided low-level support for new fuel and a modest circulation of air, while keeping a compact fire together (wood ignites from direct contact with other burning wood). The two uprights served to pivot a roasting spit or other cross-member on which a cooking-pot could hang.

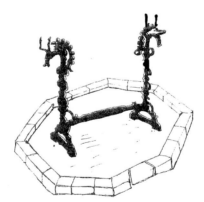

Firedogs

The reek

Reek (smoke) would be left to find its way out through the loosely assembled roof – not so far away, as the homes were only single-storey. Indeed, well into the seventeenth century it was reported of the North that 'the ordinary country houses (were) pitiful cots, built of stone, and covered with turves, having in them but one room, many of them no chimneys, the windows very small holes, and not glazed.' (John Ray travelling in East Lothian, 1662).

The modest dimensions provide a hint as to the constructive use of wood smoke – for preserving food. Ideal would be fires burning oak, beech, walnut, hazel and fruit woods (less useful: sycamore or soft woods). Offcuts ('spiles') from the everyday carpentry of early times would be best. Peat, on higher moorlands, could serve equally well.

Today smoking food is reckoned a specialist task, but back in the Middle Ages it was a process available to everyone in their own homes. Our common word 'pudding' seems to derive from the animal stomach or intestines into which ingredients would be stuffed to make a traditional haggis or sausage for smoking. In the rafters above each hearth, where the smoke collected, would surely hang a stick of herring, a string or two of sausages or a ham, putting to good use what would seem to us the main disadvantage of early house design. The broad chimneys of Tudor buildings would be equally useful for smoking; but no one in later times would care to have their food preserved and flavoured by coal or coke fumes!

Ridding

One aspect of the open, central wood fire worth noting is the infrequency with which the hearth would need to be cleaned. Keeping a fire going continuously rather than stopping and cleaning it out regularly would be an obvious advantage and it seems that ash was left to accumulate as long as practical. As Lawrence Wright points out, 'The ash must be kept deep upon the hearth, as a reservoir of heat.' (Wright, 1964, p.10) It was usual 'to let the wood ash accumulate on the open fire until the fire itself was burning a foot or two above the floor-level.' (Allingham, 1909, pp.113–4). Practically, before the invention of matches, no one would wilfully want a fire to go out. Whether it was possible to leave the hearth to one annual clearing up is uncertain, but the tradition certainly developed of ritually disassembling the fire, cleaning the hearth and rekindling the fire anew on a special day each year.

In the South this was at Easter (hence 'Spring Cleaning') – reflecting the tradition (from the Roman calendar and the Christian Church) that the New Year began in March. In the North it was a mid-winter affair associated with Viking-like fondness for fire festivals and celebrating the New Year at the end of December. Here is an account of the New Year's Eve customs in East Durham (1930s), described by Margaret Reed of Seaham:

> There was a lot of preparation… A special shop for a start – if there was any money left over from Christmas. Our best supper was an ox tongue with pease pudding, but there would also be freshly baked mince pies and so on, depending on funds. From morn till midnight, everything was geared to welcoming in the New Year. Everything that could be polished, scrubbed or cleaned was brightened up. The floors would all be swept – to get rid of the year's accumulation, as it were. For us children, the treat was being allowed to stay up. We were bathed, and dressed in our 'second best' – not quite the very best, but smart enough…

> By 9 pm, the fires would have been let to go out, then the ashes cleared out, and the cold grates left ready to receive new fire… About ten to twelve, our father would set out, with some coals and sticks (kindling) with him – to make sure (on return) there would always be fire in your hearth for the coming year. All the family men would gather at

the bottom of the street, and await midnight. The New Year would be signalled by the church bells ringing and the ships in harbour would blow their whistles, the pits too, while we waited silent indoors for the first footer. This would be our own father of course.

The fire would be lit, all the doors to the rooms through the house opened, everyone within wished a Happy New Year! There would be a little cake and a drink; the front door would be left open for any callers and people would go round and visit, but especially family. I think it was during the War that it became less of a family occasion, more of a general gesture of goodwill to your friends and so on.

Conditions had changed remarkably from wood-burning hearth in a cottage to coal fire in a mining terrace house, but this ritual rekindling of the fires is only explicable in terms of the practices of the Medieval hearth and its olden-time wood fire.

For the younger (post-war) generation, the New Year has symbolised a looser sense of conviviality. Charles Trelogan reports from New Herrington, near Sunderland:

On New Year's Eve the fire was cleared of all the ashes – 'a clean start for the New Year'. The first footer would carry a piece of coal to place on the burning or newly cleaned fire. Also front doors were left open so that the convivial caller could come in for a drink.

The fireside

A gradual but important change during the Middle Ages was the move of the fireplace from the centre to the side of the room, at the wall. This was essential in better two-storey buildings, as the main room would be on the first floor and you would be ill-advised to light a fire on the wooden floorboards. The walls of taller buildings, whether bastles, castles, peel towers or manor house, would be of stone, into which a suitable flag base for a fire could be easily set. This new arrangement was later found convenient in single-storey stone cottages (at one end) or long-houses (fires back-to-back at a central wall) and had the advantage that smoke could be channelled outside through a simple flue.

Such flues were initially plain vents for smoke, and not yet intended to create updraughts; tall chimneys are not needed for wood fires. The typical Tudor fireplace for burning wood would be a broad space, so as to accommodate logs of varying sizes (saving on the amount and accuracy of sawing or chopping needed), plus space at the side for a pile of new wood to dry, ready for use.

Such wide fireplaces would ideally double in function for heating and cooking unless a separate kitchen was available. The exaggerated 'hood' of the broad fireplace provided a new resource for smoking food. If the flues needed occasional scraping, a bairn was considered ideal for the task; and the soot obtained would by no means be wasted: mixed with gum arabic, it made our earliest black ink. The large Tudor fireplace is associated inevitably with succulent joints of meat roasted on a spit. If the heat came from one fixed direction (i.e. below), the meat could only be cooked evenly by the ruse of keeping the joint turning. Spit-roasting is still possible with a 'rotisserie', though hardly on the scale of a Tudor banquet, whole ox or whatever. (Well, a whole ox is traditional at the Houghton Feast in Co. Durham if you want to find out how it's done.)

Here is a description of a simple case of open fire roasting from Scotland, first half of the nineteenth century:

> In a few minutes Grizzie entered, carrying a fowl just killed, its head as she came all but dragging on the ground at the end of its long, limp neck. She seated herself on a stool, somewhere about the middle of the large space of the kitchen floor and proceeded to pluck and otherwise prepare it for the fire. Having last of all split it open from end to end, so turning it into something not unlike an heraldic double eagle, she approached the fire, the fowl in one hand, the gridiron in the other...
>
> (G. MacDonald, *Castle Warlock*, ch. 15)

Peat fires

Useful peat could be cut in many upland areas, and forms something of a special case: a peat fire could require a 'wind hearth', that is with a hollow below so that bellows could introduce extra air to make the peat red-hot. Generally, peat burned slowly and with low heat, but had advantages: "The turf fires were famous and when well-made, with a wet turf pushed into the ashes and a scuttle of turf mould thrown on, they kept in overnight. Many people, especially innkeepers of the moorland inns, claimed that their fires had not been out for a hundred years." (Hartley, 1972, p.11) Like other open fires, cooking tended to be in simple pots hung over the fire: "Although some houses had bread ovens, and bread was also baked by placing dough on the hot turf ashes, the characteristic cooking in the moorland houses and cottages was by means of a variety of pans over a turf or peat fire; this continued long after ranges were installed, well into the 1930s, until this type of fuel ceased to be harvested." (Hartley, 1972, p.13)

The peat smoke undoubtedly added a special dimension to the flavour of the food. This is hard to recapture, but here is a recipe:

Turf cakes

1 lb flour / 3–4 oz. lard, a bit salt, 1 tisp baking powder, $^1/_2$ cup of cream or milk.

"Baked as one cake in a large frying pan with a lid on, they were about half an inch thick and were turned with a knife and cloth after five minutes." (Hartley, 1972, p.15)

The switch to coal

Coal became more available and its advantages more widely appreciated in cities like London from the sixteenth century on. In all big towns wood was a relatively scarce and expensive commodity – it would have to be transported in for a start and the priority claim was for timber for ship-building, house-building and other serious carpentry needs. For industrial processes too, coal made a better and more available source of heat than wood-based charcoal. Using transport by sea, it became economic to ship coal to London and this according to Daniel Defoe was the origin of the term 'sea-coal'.

In King James I reign, "the fore said sea-cole and pitt cole is become the general fewell of this Britaine Island, used in the houses of the nobilitie, cleargy, and gentrie in London and in all other cityes and shires of the Kingdom as well as for dresing of meate, washing, brewing, dying and otherwise." (*HRCM*, ch.1)

Coal radiates more heat than wood and so makes a more efficient heating and cooking fuel – but has special needs that radically influenced house design. It required a fireplace at the wall and walls (or at least a surround) of stone or brick; a flue to the outside (for the truly noxious fumes); and for that flue to be extended upwards in the form of a chimney to provide sufficient updraught to draw away any carbon monoxide and other gas products and to draw in oxygen at the base to help the coal ignite and continue burning; exact figures we lack, as the temperature for the ignition of coal varies with its carbon content. The point is, to maximise the flow of air, a narrow fireplace and flue was favoured coupled with a lofty chimney. Neglecting this, we learn "Queen Eleanore was forced to leave Nottingham Castle where she was staying in 1257, on account of the objectionable smoke produced by the burning of sea coal." (*HRCM*, ch.1)

An iron grate of some kind to lift the fire up helped increase the access to oxygen by directing the updraught through the body of the fire, as did use of a set of bellows or a 'blazer' or 'bleezer' – a metal screen that could

Early fire grate

be held across the fireplace-opening to channel the draught. The fireplace for a coal fire is ideally narrow and modest of scale. If wider old-style fireplaces were to be adapted to coal, a smaller grate would be set centrally, often a sort of lattice box of wrought iron, or perhaps some of the space would be bricked in. "Coal needs to be contained in a compact mass so that enough heat will be generated for its combustion." (Eveleigh, 1983, p.3)

The 'great rebuilding', which saw smaller farmsteads and cottages replaced with 'modern' two-storey brick farmhouses is reckoned to have occurred later here than in the South. In the North East it was a movement typical of the seventeenth century, when securer leases and longer tenures encouraged tenants to invest in 'new build' which would serve for generations to come. Stone continued to be used, though brick was gaining in popularity – initially imported from Holland as ballast in collier ships. Single-storey rubble-stone houses were now likelier to be labourers' cottages or used for storage than to form the farmhouse proper.

Unlike the token or non-chimneys of the wood fire age, the chimneys for coal fires could not be disguised or overlooked and this made the unit of the fireplace an ideal basis for levying a seventeenth century tax, known as the Hearth Tax. From the records of the tax we learn, for example, that in 1664 Dawdon in East Durham had one building with 17 hearths (surely the now ruinous fortification and demolished manor house known as Dalden Tower), one building with two hearths (a farmhouse? The minister's home?) and six buildings with just one hearth (presumably labourers' or small-holders' cottages). The Age of Coal had arrived, with its own social distinctions and markers of status.

Using a coal fire

Clinker and ash would need to be cleared out regularly from below the grate of a coal fire to ensure the passage of a good current of air. In view of the intense heat generated, this could only be partially done while the fire was alight. Once a day or once a week, the coal fire would need to be left to die out and a thorough cleaning undertaken – but the extra work was likely to seem worth the improved radiating heat that a well-managed coal fire can provide.

In place of free-standing firedogs to suspend cooking vessels from, a branch or iron rod could be lodged across the flue opening, and pots could hang from that, using a chain and 'S' hook to vary the height. According to Heslop, a 'galley-baak' was 'the balk or beam fixed across a chimney over the fire... The galley-baak was sometimes a tree branch with the bark stripped off, but otherwise undressed and unsquared. In this case it was commonly called a 'peeled grain'.

"(An) early method of holding pots and cauldrons over the fire was to suspend them from a chain or pot-hook hanging from a cross-beam in the chimney. The chain consisted of large, round or elongated links and the pots were hooked to it and the hanging point adjusted by means of a simple 'S'-type hook." (Tibbott, 1982, p.12)

Height adjustment could be made alternately by using a vertical strip of metal with notches to seat hooks; this was called a 'rackin' (i.e. racheting) crook. Horizontal movement was possible if a 'crane' was used, anchored in front of and to one side of the fire: "By swinging it, the suspended pot could be held in position above the fire, or moved away from it…" (Tibbott, 1982, p.13) In a more graphic image, Beatrix Potter describes how Tom Kitten "jumped right up into the fireplace, balancing himself upon the iron bar where the kettle hangs."

Utensils

The kitchen was (and is) much more than a source of fire for cooking:

> The kitchen, in the smaller cottages, is, of course, living-room and kitchen combined, generally spanned by a huge oak beam. Above the mantlepiece runs a rack for the long, bright spits used with the wood fires and sometimes the elaborate clockwork apparatus, for turning the spit, is still to be seen. The old oak dresser, bright with its china and pewter, the latter all too rare now, is the best furniture for the kitchen and with the well-scrubbed table and wooden chairs, just fit in the general scheme.
>
> (Allingham, 1909, p.123)

Some idea of the range of cooking utensils and kitchen equipment can be obtained from notices of auctions in the local press of old. Here is a list of kitchen and pantry goods, related to open fire cooking, from the one house at Guisborough, via an auction notice in the *Middlesbrough Weekly News*, 19 May, 1860: "2 dressers containing a quantity of drawers… kitchen table, 4 trays… metal tea and coffee pot, fender and fire irons, brass and tin candlesticks, 2 fire guards, meat jack, flour tin, dish covers, flour cask, jars, meat safe… plates, dishes, etc… shredding knife, scales and weights, 7 pans of various sizes, 2 frying pans, gridiron, water tins, small barrel churn, table, meat hastener, large wine bin, dripping tins, pickle tub…"

The cooking facilities an open fire provided might seem crude by modern standards, but were versatile enough, adapted to both 'flat' foods and liquids.

Basic would be a metal pot or cauldron for stew or for boiling water to cook in – like earlier pottery vessels that were thrown on a wheel, it had a rounded body and rounded bottom. Practically, this helped heat spread more evenly round the vessel when it was set over the fire. In the kitchen of Michael Jeffreyson of Darlington, 1612, were found "a paire of great rackes, a drippin pane, a reckincroke, a cauldon & a kettle, a maskefatt [for infusing or perhaps brewing], a cooling tub, a draftub, a [sae tub], two skeles [pails] & a litle bordd [table], iii seckes and two pooks [bags]". (*Surtees Society*, vol.201, no.32)

A typical cauldron would be made of metal, cast in one piece; they were still standard ware in Scotland in the mid-nineteenth century for making broth. (Eveleigh, 1986, p.17) Sometimes the cauldron had three stubby legs to give it more stability when set on the ground. This type was more usually called a 'yetling'. A smaller pan with three short legs and a long handle was known as a 'skillet'. (A long handle is a sure sign of a cooking utensil designed for the open fire!)

For flat goods such as oatcakes, a bakestone was the earliest support, placed directly by or in the open fire. "In Wales and the Pennines, flat oatcakes were baked on a bakestone, a heated stone slab placed on the hearth." (Eveleigh, 1986, p.28) The bakestone or 'backstone' was a flat, thin stone slab on the edge of the fire, used "for baking unleavened cakes upon, before iron plates were used... Stones are still in use for oatcakes." (Brockett, Newcastle, 1830s)

Dutch oven

In due course, a metal griddle took the place of the stone slab: "griddles or girdles (are) thick circular plates of iron, usually about 12 inches diameter." (Eveleigh, 1986, p.28) It was an ideal surface for cooking oatcakes (large or small) and similar flat grain-based products on. The oatcake was also amenable to being part-cooked and then stored for later re-heating. How? "A fleak in Yorkshire is something resembling a gate suspended horizontally a foot or two from the top of a room, and bearing the bread and cheese and bacon of the family." (Raine, 1837, p.ccccxxix) Or in Brockett's definition "flaik, flake – a wooden frame at the top of a kitchen for keeping oatcakes upon." Secure from rodents if not from smoke and other kitchen stithe, these part-cooked oatcakes would be conveniently available for re-use at any time by toasting at the fire. As Florence White notes: "It must be crisped quickly before it is to be eaten." (*Good things*, p.78)

An enterprising way of cooking with an open fire was the so-called 'dutch oven', used from the early eighteenth century on: "they were made of tinplate and stood in front of [i.e. facing] the fire, the bright surface reflecting the heat, reducing cooking time and saving fuel." (Eveleigh, 1986, p.21) Reputedly, it was a tasty way of cooking bacon. "We all had our home-fed bacon and a Dutch oven used to fix onto the front of the bars of the fire and there were prongs out where they used to put the rashers of bacon on and the fat and grease used to fall into the bottom." (Cawson and Kibblesworth via Beamish, 1993/5) (For a story of a dutch oven and its bacon, see Part four.)

Though fires and fireplaces had come a long way in a few centuries, the cooking process remained much the same. Whether from wood or coal, the heat was more or less directly transferred to the food. Exceptionally small items could be wrapped and cooked in the hot wood embers, to simulate oven cooking, but cooking on an open fire remained in general a uni-dimensional affair and limited in that the source of heat could not be speedily adjusted: you needed to set your pan nearer to or further from the heat, your cooking vessel higher or lower – thankfully a large cauldron was unlikely to 'boil over'.

Diet

An additional limitation would be the range of ingredients available, hence the importance of the cottage garth, aka kitchen garden, aka allotment. A discouragement here was that rural jobs were seasonal and the tenure of a labourer's cottage often short-term, so that there was little incitement to maintain a cottage or work its garden under such circumstances. (This was the theme of *Description of the County of Northumberland*, ca.1812.)

For those with low income who lived away from the main centres of trade and communication, the countryside may have seemed less than idyllic. In 1810 John Bailey reported of agricultural labourers in Co. Durham:

> The food and mode of living of the labouring classes are very simple: the bread generally used is made of maslin [mixed grain flour], leavened and baked in loaves, called brown bread; the most usual breakfast is bread and milk and in winter when the latter is scarce, hasty pudding or crowdy is substituted for it; for dinner, pudding, or dumpling and potatoes, with a small portion of animal food, or bread and cheese, with milk and very often bread and milk only; for supper, bread and milk, or potatoes and milk and when the latter is scarce, treacle beer is used in its stead.

The foods were basically organic, local and seasonal. The more isolated your dwelling (e.g. in the Dales in the west of our region), the more self-sufficient you would need to be. The basis of the diet was carbohydrates – grain, potatoes, turnips; while protein and fat was provided by a small amount of animal food and milk or cheese. Green vegetables are seldom mentioned, though they were surely grown and would be an important contribution to what we recognise as a balanced diet – beans and peas had been in cultivation since Anglo-Saxon times; the greens associated with growing other vegetables would not be wasted, e.g. sprout tops. Cabbage was perhaps commonest, since 'kale-pot' (literally cabbage pot) was the standard name for a stew pot. This is evidenced in the border ballad *The Battle of Otterbourne*:

> The Otterbourne's a bonnie burn;
> 'Tis pleasant there to be;
> But there is nought at Otterbourne
> To fend [provide for] my men and me.
>
> The deer rins wild on hill and dale
> The birds fly wild from tree to tree;
> But there is neither bread nor kale
> To fend my men and me...

The kale-pot

> At noon, when frae yor daily toil
> Yor freed te dine – the pot i' boil
> Wi' broth, at hyem [home], yor heart 'ill cheer,
> Gud dinners myek the hoose mair *dear*,
> But broth, withoot thor's plenty peas
> An' barley i' them, seldum please;
> For barley, peas,– green, whole, an' splet,–
> Cum te maw shop, the best ye'll get.
>
> (Joe Wilson)

One of the basic arts of cooking over an open fire – so traditional as to be virtually prehistoric – was broth or stew in a cauldron-shaped cooking-pot. (A traditional standard and by no means the preserve of witches. Notwithstanding Joe Wilson's "Aw've seen her gurn [grin] just like one o' Macbeth's witches roond the kyel-pot.")

Today a large saucepan or a casserole is used for preference, but the term kale-pot endured well into the nineteenth century.

The name 'kale pot' contains a hint as to the importance in the olden-time diet of the green cabbage:

And of course, the greens, you always had cabbages because, in the allotment they used to plant them, the different types of cabbages, to come different times. And I can always, remember, like, there was spring cabbages, I used to like them best of all, that was the lovely green ones, still get them now, and the sprouts in the winter time, but during the summer they used to have cauliflowers. And they used to get this curly cabbage and different stuff like that. But it was always good, plenty of veg to be got – that was one thing, you always had any amount of veg, which was good for you.

George Patterson (Beamish, 2004/61)

While potatoes were more easily got from the farmer:

Why you could go to the farmer any time, and especially the hind that used to live up in the buildings farm, fella called Trotter. And we used to go up there wi' a bucket, and said, 'Can we have a bucket o' potatoes, Mr. Trotter?' And he used to say, aye, and, mebbies tuppence. You would give him tuppence there for a big bucket of lovely potatoes, you know, home grown. By, they used to be tasty as well, like balls of flour when they were cooked. And that's where we used to get [them], or, [the] majority o' them.

(*ibid.*)

Broth was the simplest meal that could be cooked in a kale-pot and had the added advantage that it could be made in a large quantity, left to simmer, used when needed and then topped up and reheated for late-comers. Within reason, it provided a continuous source of nourishing food – and an oatcake or flat stottie was the ideal accompaniment, to dip in or wipe the bowl clean with afterwards. "With the broth were slabs of yester cake – flat, circular pieces of dough baked with the loaves." (Hitchin, 1962, p.20)

Well into the 1950s, it served as a symbol of sociability, as Tom Moreland records:

There was a positive side to this disreputable part of Seaham [i.e. Dawdon] in that people never seemed to lock their doors. They also looked out for each other. I have no recollection of any house in the area ever being burgled.

If someone was in bother their neighbours came, not to be nosy but to see how they could be of help. This comradeship was born out of necessity; you could be desperate for their help on the morrow. The coal mining industry took no prisoners – it was sink or swim. Good neighbours could help you pull on the oars of life.

There was more than one time when, on returning from holiday, the fire was burning with a cheery glow, and a pot of stew was on the stove waiting to welcome us home.

And if being economical and simple to make and sociable was not enough, it was also good for you:

Brose – barley broth:

Eat your brose, barley brose,

And when ye're an aad, aad wifie

Ye'll still can touch your toes.

Brose (in Welsh 'brwes') is alternately conceived of as "a dish of crushed oatcake steeped in salt beef or bacon stock." (Tibbott, 1982, p.8)

One peculiarity of broth is that it is used in the North East as if it were a plural noun – 'a few broth' is the standard term. So here are a few:

Basic broth

The standard ingredients would be water, salt, thrifty vegetables and perhaps whole barley. Meat might be a luxury in such a pot (hence the saying 'men will sometimes (be lucky enough to) eat the bacon with the bean', but the gentle cooking of salted meat (soaked beforehand) would suit the kale-pot well enough. "Fresh vegetables and bones were the main ingredients, but bits of meat floated around on the surface and suet dumplings bobbed up here and there or lay hidden in the savoury depths." (Hitchin, 1962, p.20) In James Weams' song, *The neighbours doon belaa* "…(will) borrow yer onions, leeks and peas, whenever there's pots te boil."

Joseph Parker noted a typical cottager's meal (in the Corbridge/Haltwhistle area at the end of the nineteenth century) as "the shank end of a neck o' mutton and lots of brown potatoes, and a quart of well water." (1896, p.57) That would hardly satisfy us today, so here is the mid-twentieth century version (from Margaret Reed, Seaham):

Into the broth pan would go a piece of brisket or a ham shank, along with a penny-worth or two of pot-stuff (barley, lentils, split peas, [and probably butter-beans]) and a selection of root vegetables (leeks, carrots, turnips, parsnips, and possibly grated potato to thicken the liquid) – whatever was available or could be afforded. Cabbage might be cooked and served separately. Dumplings were a much appreciated addition! On the first day, the stew would be eaten hot and some of the meat, all the dumplings and the tasty liquor consumed. On the second day, remaining meat would be eaten cold, perhaps with beetroot or the like…

The nearest equivalent today would be a casserole or a stew, but there are many possibilities: vegetables cooked in stock, then creamed in a liquidiser, give a fine and healthy modern-day soup; or with chunks of vegetable in place, make the base of a good vegetable curry.

A Welsh version of kale (*cawl*) might comprise "a large piece of salted bacon or salted beef boiled in an iron cauldron or large saucepan, with potatoes and any other available vegetables added." (Tibbott, 1982, p.8)

But in the North East, the emphasis was on economy:

> And then he used to sell these ham shanks as well for, you used to only pay threppence for a ham shank. And [we] used to boil them and [we] would stick carrots and parsnips and all sorts in it, potatoes and everything like that, and have a hell of a basin of broth, you know, wi' big lumps of this ham shank in. But you weren't bothered about the meat because you got the flavour out of the ham shank. I've seen me mother mek a one with the ham, then she would lift the ham shank out and she would keep that.
>
> George Patterson (Beamish, 2004/61)

> Sheeps' Heed Broth – a sheep's head cost four old pennies then. My Mother might say 'Had away to the butchers and get me a sheep's heed, and tell him to cut it as near the tail as possible!' She would have to skin it, then split it in half, take eyes out and brains (brains would be cooked separately, and served on toast). Then boil the rest of the head, including the jaw and teeth – with some carrot, turnip, leeks, peas (all from our allotment) and a little barley. My Mother's broth was good – you could stand a spoon up in it, it was that thick, not watter!
>
> (F.M., Ashington)

Of course, the kale-pot was not limited to broths or savouries: "The large pan could also be used for steaming – a pot pie of steak and kidney in a bowl lined with suet – or a round suet pudding with dates and figs, boiled in a cloth, and served with a white sauce." (M.R.) A typical 'sweet' would be just such a boiled suet pudding with figs, dried apricots, or currants to give flavour – served with a white sauce or custard. In earlier days, the luxury of a 'figgy pudding' would be something reserved for Christmas!

A popular vegetable dish, steamed or boiled, remains:

Leak pudding

8 oz plain flour / 4 oz suet / 1/2 tisp salt / 1 tisp baking powder / 1 lb leeks, cleaned and roughly chopped.

Mix all together into a dough with water; put in a greased basin and cover; steam for 2 hours. (*Story of Seaham Collection*)

Another recipe

8 oz self-raising flour / 4 oz suet / 1 level tisp salt / 6 oz leeks, prepared and chopped / water to mix.

Mix to a firm dough. Roll out into an oblong, fill with chopped, seasoned leeks. Roll up and tie into a floured cloth. Boil for 1 1/2 hours. (*N'd Cook Book*)

An account of the making:

> A leek pudding would be made up, then stood on a pudding clout, and the corners of it gathered up and tied on top. Unlike the steak 'n' kidney pie, the leek pudding would be placed in boiling water direct. It would be served to accompany meat, with gravy poured over the leek pudding.
>
> (F.M., Ashington)

> In 'clubland' Leek Show Monday used to be a tradition when leek broth was made for the members from the leeks in the show. Many used to 'be idle' that day and celebrate in the club.
>
> (Dave Neville)

A problem with green vegetables is that they do not keep or travel well. Most such would be grown for immediate personal or at least local use. Hence the advantage of the local allotment:

> Me father used to grow cucumbers on his muckheap and, er, he had a bit of a lay-too, for his greenhouse thing where he used to grow his tomatoes. He had tomatoes and cucumbers. He always had lettuce all the year round 'cos he used to plant them every fortnight. And when [new lettuce] was comin' up he just used to pull the others and feed them to the hens; there was nothing wasted, everything had its cycle there and it just used to go round.
>
> George Patterson (Beamish, 2004/61)

Desirable as freshness is, garden products capable of being dried and stored were just as important. Thus Henryson's poem on the town and country mouse fable has the country mouse feasting on 'beinis and nuttis, peis, ry and quheit' (beans, nuts, pease, rye, wheat) when she comes to town – surely a guide to the well-stocked (Scottish) store-room. A modern packet of 'broth mix' might contain red lentils, pearl barley, yellow split peas, green split peas and barley flakes, but a special place in the recipe books belongs to the solo pea:

Pease pudding

Use the water a ham shank was cooked in, or boil the peas in the same pan as your ham joint.

Put the split yellow peas (not lentils) in a muslin bag, allowing room for expansion and boil for some 2 hours till soft.

Carlins

The name comes either from Care Sunday (in Lent) or 'carlin' (an old woman, the sort that needed caring for). The dish was traditionally set out on pub counters for customers to help themselves, at the appropriate season. The problem today could be finding the carlins themselves (the peas that is), as a special brand of grey dried peas ('only grey or maple peas') is proper to the recipe.

From Jack Gair: "Soak the carlins overnight in water, drain and place in a pan of boiling water and cook for approx 20 minutes but make sure the carlins are not 'mushy'. Drain the carlins [make sure they are dry!] and fry for 2 or 3 minutes in the butter. Serve them with brown sugar. It was said that when served in pubs a dash of rum was added... Carlins were cooked and eaten on their own – lots of public houses and working men's clubs gave them out for free."

Instead of sugar, they could be served with vinegar (one correspondent remembers them as "unexciting grey peas we ate with vinegar.") You ate them with your fingers, by the way.

The turnip

An important food source in the agricultural era (and especially in the age of farm improvement, the seventeenth–eighteenth centuries) was the turnip, which fulfilled a dual role as animal and human food. Bulk was an important advantage and nutritional value, but mainly the turnip was esteemed as an autumn root crop suitable for storage, that could sustain cattle (and human) through the winter months. In a Scottish winter and no doubt in the North East too, you were likely to find your milk 'scanty and tasting not a little of turnip.' (MacDonald, *Castle Warlock*, ch. 17)

Snagger (for harvesting neeps, etc.)

Curiously, whereas potato has only one dialect by-name – 'tatie' – turnip has a host of variant names locally, which attest its role as a prime crop and essential foodstuff throughout the North East. For the range of names, see the Glossary section.

The practical (as well as verbal) importance of the turnip to domestic economy can be judged from the following snippet, relating to the miners' strike in April 1840:

> In consequence of the depredations committed in potato and turnip fields during the night, watchers were engaged in many places to protect the property...
>
> (Latimer, 1857)

No songs in praise of the turnip have survived, but here are two short anecdotes about the fondness for turnips, from the 1930s...

> And then you never paid for turnips. I mean, all the turnip fields that was round. When it come to choppin' time, you could always gan to the farm and they would give yer one, because they used to lead them in as well and, they used to stack them up for the beasts, and the cows.
>
> George Patterson (Beamish, 2004/61)

> Turnips. We caal'd 'em snarters of course. An' it was up the lonnin, an' yi knaa ye've got the dyke side which is the hedge raa, that was wheer we sat and ate the snarters after the deed was deun. The idea o' putting the thrippenny bits in the holes for the turnips was the strange thing. That was me Mam's idea.
>
> Nae fence, the field was open wi' a cart track – thor wuz just whole fields o' turnips stretchin' for acres. An' mi Mother, she went an picked two o' them, not g'eat-big tho', so we cud eat them. She jis howked them out, an' popped the money in the hole. It was lang afore the war.
>
> Why eat them raw? Ye dee (do), thor canny when yi catch 'em fresh oot o' th' earth – them was on'y like haaf graan, yi peel'd 'em, an' ate 'em like that, sweet an' tasty, Ah'm tellin' ye.
>
> (G.P., Seaham)

If you dinnut care to eat them raw, then "mashed turnips and bacon, with a little of bacon fat poured over the turnips" is recalled by Joan Phillips (Cullercoats) or here is a way to combine them with tasty taties:

Tatie 'n' tormit toppin

Peel and roughly cube a turnip, set it to boil in plenty of salted water. Peel and cube a similar amount (or more) of potatoes, add them to the pot to boil once the turnips have had about 10 minutes' start. Boil for about 20 minutes till soft. Drain and mash (adding a little butter, milk, pepper to taste).

Eat hot with your meal, or use as a topping for shepherd's pie.

Distribution

Vegetables are much vaunted as good for you (vitamins *and* roughage), but there would be little variety for the average labourer in the early nineteenth century. Improvement, curiously, came through the very growth of urban populations. This encouraged not only market gardening in the countryside around large towns, but ultimately brought about a retailing revolution, through the development of large covered markets in the cities, while improved communication (railways!) meant food could be quickly transported. The Co-operative movement – strong in the

North East in the 1890s and 1900s – ensured combined economy and quality, e.g. they milled their own flour. That they also marketed their own brand of biscuits may have discouraged the making of these at home, but on the whole their range of ingredients were a boon and encouragement to the housewife-cook.

Another major flour producer of this period, near the Tyne Quays, was Thomas Bell whose 'Bells Royal' self-raising flour (later 'Be-Ro') became a major promotion of the 1920s. The Be-Ro recipe book, which embodies the brand, was first produced in 1923 and was handed out free at exhibitions and door-to-door – over 38 million copies are said to have been distributed.

As well as the 'store', there were any number of local shops:

> In those days there were just little village shops. All the villages. A lot of the shops in those days were just in the house themselves you know. In the colliery row somebody would start up a shop you know and just put a few sweet boxes in the window or something like that. There was quite a lot in the colliery villages. Another interesting thing was as I say, you couldn't buy anything unless you went to Newcastle or somewhere such as if you wanted furniture or something like that you know.
>
> Agar (Beamish, 1984/253)

There was the added convenience for the consumer that many foodstuffs would be carted round the back-lanes ('lonnens') for sale:

> A lot of food was delivered, by local sellers coming to the back door. There was a lady from Sunderland who carried a basket of crabs and sometimes a lobster or two, on her head. She had a *Persil*-white apron and a black shawl. Then there were men with a small pony and trap selling herrings. Six a penny, they would call out; but as the day wore on, you would often hear 'twelve a penny', as they needed to sell the catch that day. There was also a vegetable seller, but he had a more substantial cart and bigger horse: there was a large set of scales to weigh the produce. And fish vans, and milk and so on…
>
> Sometimes, as children, we would be sent to the farm for a little extra milk, taking a can for a gill or two with us. The dare was to swing the can round once it was full of milk, as you spun round and round, without spilling the milk, if you could!
>
> (M.R.)

An important role would be played by small farms specialising in perishable vegetable and dairy produce to supply neighbouring towns. Farms are not places that industry has missed – they are essential to servicing the workers and their families and in turn, miners' wives would serve as casual labour at harvest time (potato and turnip and pea and bean harvests). Improvements in land drainage and the use of lime for fertiliser, the breeding of better strains of crops and more food-worthy varieties of animals in the eighteenth century was surely a precondition for the Industrial Revolution. Some farmers undoubtedly fared well: in North Yorkshire "Every farmhouse had, as some still have, a long scrubbed kitchen table with forms at either side, a grandfather clock, an oak chest, and an oak dresser with a rack locally made." (Hartley 1972 p.11) The essentials, in Trimdon, are recalled as "a big wooden kitchen table with forms (benches)." (E.J.)

Urban-industrial life had some serious defects – notably poor hygiene and high levels of disease, but gradually quality and quantity of food improved throughout the nineteenth century, both in terms of domestic production and a variety of imported (especially dried) foodstuffs – the Seaham Harbour Dock Act of 1898 includes a list of duties chargeable on the following commodities (selected edibles):

> Aerated waters, ale, beer, porter or cider, apples, arrowroot, bacon, barley, beans, beef, biscuits, biscuits (fancy), bread, butter, cabbage (see vegetables), cattle (calves, sheep, lambs and pigs, horses, oxen and cows), cheese, cocoa, coffee, confectionery, corn (Indian) or maize, cranberries, currants, drugs, eggs, fat, farina (starch), fish, figs, flour or meal, fowls, fruit (dried), herrings (see fish), hops, juice (lime) (see wine), kernels (palm or ground nut), lard, macaroni, malt, maize, mineral waters, molasses, mustard, nuts, oats or oatmeal, onions, oranges and lemons, peas, pepper, pears, potatoes, pork, provisions, provisions (preserved), raisins, rabbit, rice, rum (see wines and spirits), salt (white), salt (rock), sago, semolina, spices, sugar, tapioca, tea, turnips (see veg.), vegetables, vegetables (preserved in tins), vegetables (compressed), vermicelli, vinegar, wheat, whiting, wines and spirits.

No wonder an improvement on open fire cooking was developed to parallel this opportunity. However, first:

Meat in the diet

Meat would play a limited part in the common diet. With few means of preserving meat (except salting or smoking), large animals would scarcely be worth killing for family use: the beasts would go to market for the town butchers to divide and sell. In earlier times, it was more practical to cull animals in the autumn – in recognition of the poor resources for feeding animals during the winter. As opposed to food animals, important draught animals like the ox (yielding to the horse only in the eighteenth century) were to be kept alive at all costs. If your herd of one suffered a mortal accident, it was an economic disaster, and the knacker's man was to be called in as quickly as possible to make the best of the situation. This is the theme of one of the earliest printed dialect texts – *Yorkshire dialogue between an awd wife, a lass, and a butcher*, 1673, and the importance of the task is conveyed through the butcher's elaborate preparations:

He'll come <u>belive</u>, or <u>aibles titter</u>,   soon / even sooner

For when he <u>hard</u> i' what a <u>twitter</u>	heard / bad state
Your poor <u>owse</u> lay, he took his flail	ox
An' hang'd 't by t' <u>swipple</u> on a nail;	flap-end

An' <u>teuk</u> a <u>mell</u> from fra t' top o' t' <u>wharns</u>   took / hammer / querns

An' sware he'd <u>ding</u> your <u>owse</u> i' t' <u>harns</u>.   hit / ox / brains

He stack his shak-fork up i' t' <u>esins</u>   eaves

An' teuk his mittens, reached his <u>bill</u>,   chopper

An' off o' t' <u>yune-head</u> teuk a swill   oven-top / bucket

To <u>kep</u> t' owse blude in. Leuk, he's coom!'   catch

'Than reach a <u>thivel</u> or <u>strum</u>   types of stick

To stir his blude; stand not to tauk…

The 'owse blude' or ox blood is apparently to be discarded in the poem; but the awd wife would surely want it to make black pudding. The essential ingredient of black pudding in the modern day is fresh pig's blood, which equally places it outside the scope of the household chef. The blood is matched with suet, diced pork fat, pre-soaked oatmeal and pre-boiled barley. For extra flavour, some soft-fried onion and a little salt, ground coriander, pepper and ground mace can be added. The mixture is piped into large sausage casings and poached in simmering water for about 10 minutes. For use, thick slices are fried and served as part of a 'full breakfast'.

The turnip is credited with changing the custom of a late autumn cull and effectively re-patterning the practicalities of animal farming. It was a cheap crop, easily storable, and suitable for feeding cattle through the winter months when pasture was not available. Thus Brockett wrote in the 1820s: "mairt – a cow or ox slaughtered at Martinmas and salted for winter store. The custom of salting meat to last throughout the inclement months was universal among our ancestors. Though less frequent, since the extensive cultivation of turnips, it still partially prevails in Northumberland…"

From the time of Franklin's expedition to the Arctic in 1845, canned food has had an important role to play. Early can-openers incorporated the icon of a bull's head in honour of the main donor. Corned beef (so called because it was preserved with 'corns' or grains of salt) and baked beans are two of the most enduringly popular canned products. If you want to add a little romance to their image, consider the southern United States cowboy, who came into his own after the Civil War. One of the most profitable lines then was the raising of cattle, which had to be driven on the hoof from the south-western states to Chicago (or nearer railheads), where great cattle-pens held the animals prior to slaughter and canning as corned beef, a product exported to the populous eastern states and eventually devoured worldwide. A process dependant on cowboys. When they bivouacked for the night and lit a fire and hung the universal kale-pot over it, the main ingredient in their tasty broth would be – beans. Meanwhile, in the UK mirror, the major Tyneside brand canning plant was situated at North Shields. Checked shirts and neckerchiefs remain popular in some County Durham villages.

In the Age of the Hamburger it is reassuring to know that un-minced steak was revered in olden times, as it is today. In this stanza from a well-known eighteenth/nineteenth century song (a cheeky satire on the serious border-ballad style), the skill of cooking was reduced to a good steak and griddle cake:

Can she cook a bit o' steak?

Billy Boy, Billy Boy?

Can she cook a bit o' steak, me Billy Boy?

She can cook a bit o' steak,

Aye, and myek (make) a gairdle cake

And me Nancy kittled (tickled) me fancy

Oh me charmin' Billy Boy.

Indulgence in fresh-cooked meat was something of an ambition in the early nineteenth century for the poorer classes, an almost immoral urge to ape (or democratic instinct to equal) the great institutional dinners of the privileged classes. 'Wild eating' attracted not only greedy admiration but downright snobbish disapproval:

When Adam was living, he ne'er could boast

Of partaking at tables of beef boil'd or roast,

For what record tells us, his diet was most

Locusts, wild honey, and costard;

But ower this narration aw better be brief,

It's weel knawn to the world now, it is my belief,

That coblers are getting ower fond o' roast beef,

Plumb pudding, pea pudding, and mustard…

(*Heeltap's Disaster*, Marshall, 1829)

The symbol of meat as a luxury item and feasting as a fine ambition persists, but a more practical way of fulfilling this at the household level would be the pig and chicken. It was customary in many a mining row of houses, to keep a communal pig. It could be fed on peelings and scraps, slops and spoiled food from everyone's kitchen and when it came time to kill the porker, all would get a share – a joint, some chops, bacon to cure, giblets, brain, bits for sausages, blood for savoury puddings. Nowt was wasted 'except the squeal'.

All the miners in the village had a big garden to cultivate to help with the family food bill. The only ones who hadn't gardens were the people who lived in the cross rows. Nearly everybody kept pigs or poultry… we [children] had to help look after them, going to the farm at Kibblesworth for straw. Potato peelings, cabbage leaves and meal were cooked in a big set pot and put into big barrels ready for a few days.

I remember the last pig we had was 32 stones in weight. Now when the pig was ready to kill it was killed in the backyard of the owner's house. Then it was hung up in the kitchen on special hooks that had been fixed into the wooden beams. It was cut up into joints and sold to the people in the village. One of the family used to go from door-to-door taking orders and I can tell you that home-fed pork takes some beating...

Cawson and Kibblesworth (Beamish, 1993/5)

Brawn

Pig's trotters formed a brawn. You would use the cheapest cut of beef (hough) and a couple of pig's trotters, fit them in a pan, and boil and boil them to bits. All the bone and hoof would be removed, and the meat put in a basin. A saucer that exactly fitted inside the basin would be placed on top and weighted with a brick, to press the brawn as it set.

(F.M., Ashington)

The pride generated by pig keeping is (I suspect) the un-stated subject of an unusual food song, printed in 1834 in the collection *The Bishoprick Garland*.

Up the Raw, maw bonny hinny,

Up the Raw, lass, ivvery day;

For shap an' colour, maw bonny hinny,

Thou <u>bangs</u> thy mother, maw canny bairn.   beats/surpasses

Black as a craw, maw bonny hinney,

Thou bangs them a', lass, ivvery day;

Thou's <u>a' clag-candied</u>, maw bonny hinny,   all sugar coated

Thou's double japaned, maw canny bairn.

For hide an' hue, maw bonny hinny,

Thou bangs the crew, maw canny bairn;

Up the Raw, maw bonny hinny,

Thou bangs them a', lass, ivvery day.

The beauty would end up as bacon, of course. 'Dry' curing could take place in any household or farmhouse, until the Bacon Marketing Board was set up in 1924 and a licence became necessary to kill a pig or cure some bacon. Modern bacon tends to be 'wet' cured on the Danish model (see Hartley, 1972, p.28).

The importance of the pig is underlined in the existence of special 'Pork-shops', commemorated in Joe Wilson's poem:

...the gas is brightly burnin,
   It leets up a' the street,
An' the foaks stand at the window,
   Admirin pig's meat...

Byeth sausage, pies, an' saveloys,
   Sink law i' maw esteem,
Black puddins an' white puddins, <u>tee</u>,   too
   Aw eat them <u>iv</u> a dream;   in
Pig's tripe an' <u>fry</u>, an' potted heed,   liver
   May stand the public test,
But i' the shop, – an aw'm a judge,
   The pork-shop lass's best.

A splendid account of Christmas celebrations in East Durham in the early twentieth century, by George Hitchin (*Pit-Yacker*, 1962), gives pig the ultimate accolade: "Roast pork was the main dish – seldom poultry and never turkey." (p.22)

The tendency to have poultry pecking about on the village green (or what passed for common land) is celebrated in William Egglestone's picture of Crook in 1870 – before it 'grew up':

I (yes), that wez'd time when Creyk wax'd (grew) oot ev its lad's cleyse (clothes) en gat men's, fer o' fwuyk (all folk) knows ed nee playce can be a toon ed hez pants (springs) en puddles fer duck en geese to' dabble in, en where geese gans wi' bairns, butter en breed, en hens scrat ass (ash) middens in frunt ed houses, en bairns, barf't en barelegg'd, weyd amang clarts, en where wumen fwuyk throw dish washings en chemerly (urine) oot ed front door...

In Gateshead, in the early nineteenth century, Thomas Wilson celebrated the claims of poultry in the name of the honest goose:

We're <u>gawn</u> to get a <u>geuss</u> <u>te</u> <u>morn</u>,   going / goose / tomorrow
There's nought <u>aw</u> get <u>aw</u> like se weel   I
After they're grown, wi' stubble corn,
As fat and plump as ony seal.

Aw like her stuft wi' onions best,
And roasted to a single roun',
A' nicely scrimpt frae back to breast –
Not <u>brunt</u>, but beautifully brown.   burnt

Of a' the kinds of hollow meats
That greasy <u>cuicks</u> se oft are <u>speeten</u>,   cooks / putting on a spit
There's <u>nyen</u> aw tyest that ever beats   none
A geuss, 'the <u>yess</u> o' trumps' of eaten.   ace

She myeks a real royal dish,
On <u>whilk</u> a king meet myek a <u>myel</u> –   which / meal
Aw wadn't for a better wish
Were aw <u>to morn</u> a king mysel'.   tomorrow

The odments, te, beat boil or fry,
Provided geussy be a gooden –
Eat famous in a giblet pie,
Crib'd roun' wi' coils of savory pudden.

Of course, the goose was also useful for providing quills (pens) and goosefat ("Goose grease was special – it was put on our chests in winter to protect from colds" (F.M., Ashington); and from the chicken – eggs!

Most folk would keep chickens for their eggs. A general rule was, if they did no start laying by Good Friday, they were for the pot. Mebbies the hens heard us, for when we checked on Good Friday, they had all laid!

(Silksworth)

In time, common land for chickens and geese reappeared as more clearly defined allotments (especially as provided by local councils, 1922 on, and conveying some of that ancestral sense of self-sufficiency?). However, even there the attractions of poaching persisted, among pit workers:

There is a granary beside the coke ovens, where they used to keep the feed for the gallowas, the ponies from the pit.

Some of the grain would be, shall we say, appropriated and little trails would be left through the allotments to try to tempt out the ducks and geese that were kept there. If you followed the trails, they all led to Micky Driscoll's shed, and at Christmastide you'd see plenty of duck and goose feathers mixed with the hair clippings on the shed floor.

(Hudson, 1994, pp.118–9)

Wild meat

'Game' as it is usually called, was important in all eras. Ælfric, in the late tenth century, gives a short portrait of a royal hunter (a sort of forest warden) whose job included hunting the wild boar for the table.

Hwæt gelæhtest thu?

What captured you (i.e. did you capture)?

Twegen heortas & ænne bar.

Two harts and one boar.

Hu gefencge thu hig?

How caught you them?

Heortas ic gefengc on nettum 7 bar ic ofsloh.

(The) harts I caught in nets and (the) boar I slew/struck down.

Hu wære thu dyrstig ofstikian bar?

How were you daring (enough) to spear (a) boar?

Hundas bedrifon hyne to me, & ic thær togeanes standende færlice ofstikode hyne.

(The) dogs drove it to me, and I there opposite (i.e. in waiting) standing quickly speared it.

In an early border ballad (*Johnnie Armstrong*), the sort of meat fit to be set before a king is detailed:

The Eliots and Armstrongs did convene,

They were a gallant companie –

'We'll ride and meit our lawful King,

And bring him safe to Gilnockie.

Make kinnen (rabbit) and capon (chicken) ready then,

And venison in great plantie;

We'll wellcum here our royal King;
I hope he'll dine at Gilnockie!'

Venison, certainly, continues to have a noble reputation. The deer were the real kings of the forest, the perquisite of royalty and the tasty supper of outlaws. A fine description of the skill of tracking a deer – from a poacher's point of view, the forest zones being the reserve of the King – is recorded in a Northern Middle English poem, *The Parliament of the Three Ages*. (But having once tasted venison, I doubt if I would go to the lengths of stalking and tracking my own supply.)

Deer were not the only possible prey. Wild birds were a valued, since a free source of meat and a rousing song, *The Bonny Moor Hen*, records the battle between miners in 1818 and the agents of the Bishop of Durham to maintain their freedom to shoot grouse on the moors:

Now, the times being hard and provisions being dear,
The miners were starving almost we do hear;
They had nought to depend on, so well you may ken,
But to make what they could of the bonny moor hen.

There's the fat man of Oakland and Durham the same,
Lay claim to the moors, likewise to the game;
They sent word to the miners they'd have them to ken,
They would stop them from shooting the bonny moor hen.

Oh these words they were carried to Weardale with speed,
Which made the poor miners to hang down their heads;
But sent them an answer, they would have them to ken,
They would fight till they died for their bonny moor hen...

A semi-managed role – though we now think of them as entirely wild – is accorded the rabbit, which in Norman times was almost farmed, witness place-names in Co. Durham of the 'Warren Hill' type. Commercial farming of rabbits ended in the late nineteenth century, leaving rabbits to run wild – a tempting food source!

Rabbit pie

> Rabbit pie was our standard Sunday dinner. Dad would catch a pair of rabbits; Mother would skin them, cut them up, place them in a big enamel dish (including heart and kidneys) with black pudding, onion, seasoning, cover with water and place in the oven; the fire was happed up and the rabbit left to cook overnight; a top crust would be added and cooked in the morning. I wasn't keen on this as the best bits went to the men; I usually ended up with the ribs with little or not meat on them.

(F.M., Ashington)

To hunt them with gun or snare ('sniggle') remains a regional pastime but it was a sport virtually halted by the introduction of myxomatosis in the UK in 1953. It is estimated that 99% of the rabbit population perished.

> Two lovely black eyes
>
> Oh what a surprise
>
> And only for selling
>
> Scotch hare at the Felling
>
> Two lovely black eyes.

Anne Kirkman explains: "The Felling I suppose was Felling Market – Scotch Hare in case you haven't come across it was a dead cat done up to look like and be sold as rabbit!"

The loss of rabbits on the menu made room for other game recipes:

> My mother also made a rook pie for supper at the local Golf Club when the men organised a 'rook shoot'. Just the breast of the rooks was used – the rest was discarded at the site of the shoot. My mother added black pudding and whatever best steak my Dad could spare from the rations. She always used rough puff pastry, plus stock.

(M.S., North Shields)

A similar recipe for pigeon pie has been sent in; and the use of black pudding to add to the flavour and bulk to other savoury puddings is not unusual.

The sources of meat were many, and increased with refrigerated shipments from New Zealand and Australia from the 1880s on, but there are relatively few specific recipes until the modern period. Here is a basic boiled (better steamed?) pudding:

Clootie pudding

...she used to get the steak and cut it up and put it inside them there [a suet paste shell], and then she used to wrap them in a cloth, clootie puddin' as we called them. And she used to put these in this big cauldron thing and cook them over the [fire], for about three hours. And they used to be, by, when they used to come out, the smell there when you used to cut them open, and the smell of the meat.

George Patterson (Beamish, 2004/61)

While the following is an ideal combination of beef and broon ale.

Beef stew   (adapted for a casserole)

Whatever beef you can afford, cubed, rolled in seasoned flour and lightly browned ('sealed') in a little fat in a frying-pan. Place in a saucepan with onion, carrot, leeks and (importantly) equal amounts of brown ale and water or stock to cover. Bring all ingredients to the boil, then place in a casserole, cover and bring back to simmering point in the oven. Reduce oven heat till the contents just bubble, and cook for 3–4 hours. Rest till next day, then re-cook a further 2–3 hours.

Cow heel mould   (from E.S., Seaham)

8 oz stewing steak / half a cow heel / two hard-boiled eggs.

Cut the steak into small pieces and put in a pan with the cow heel; cover with cold water and add some salt; bring to the boil and simmer slowly till tender; remove meat from the bone of the cow heel; put all meat and liquid into a bowl or mould; place hard-boiled eggs in the centre; leave to set; slice to serve.

Thriftiest of all meat products was the enduring sausage. A recipe for sausage seasoning from Shildon, Co. Durham, gives 1 oz white pepper, $1/2$ tisp clove pepper, a little ground nutmeg to 6 lb of pork. The excellent Cumberland sausage has various recipes: the main ingredient is shoulder of pork, but there can also be a quantity of belly pork and a little pork fat and/or smoked bacon. A few breadcrumbs are usually added. The seasoning, in order of decreasing quantity, is: salt, black pepper, grated nutmeg and mace.

Roast whole joints seem to have remained something of a luxury. More often a selection of cuts, easy to cook, would be sold as 'Fries':

I mean, there was a fella came there, [called] Baker. He had a shop up the top o' Richard Street and we used to go down there. Now when he first came he opened this shop out, he used to have those what they called 'fries.'

And we used to go, and you could get a threepenny fry, a sixpenny fry, a ninepenny try, a shillin' fry, one-and-six, two bob, or wharever, all gan up in threppences, like, you know.

Now for a threepenny fry, you would got a link o' sausage, a piece of black puddin', a piece o' white puddin'; you wouldn't get [much real] meat, for that, it was always just like, you know, the offal 'n that, that you'd get, [plus a] piece of liver mebbies or something on as well. But, by the time you got it home and got it fried, it made a hell of a meal. But if you went and got, say you got a shillin' fry, or a wrap-up as they called them, you'd get mebbies a piece o' steak, and mebbies a chop, six links o' sausages, two, three pieces o' black puddin', some liver; and when you gorrit home, there was enough there mebbies to feed six people, you know, that he'd given yer.

Mind you used to do well with these fries as well but, as I say, it was the cheapest cuts of meat that he used to put in. There was quite a bit of fat and gristle among it and all that, you know, this hock stuff and stuff like that. But [you] could always make a good meal win-it.

George Patterson (Beamish, 2004/61)

A rise in the price of meat in the 1880s even led to a boycott by North East housewives – they would not pay such prices when they could get good nourishing herring much cheaper!

Seafood

The days are gone when fishing cobles would set out from every small port along the East Coast to catch the shoals of herring that migrated southwards each year (from the Shetlands in May, down the coast off Peterhead, North Shields, Scarborough to Great Yarmouth in October). The herring were once a stable part of the local economy, the plentiful harvest being split and dried in the sun or preserved in salt or smoked (as kippers) for resale and local use.

Open fires also made good toast and fried kippers to a turn. Every Monday a man used to bring round boxes of the latter on a flat cart and they provided a welcome tea, even though we suffered constant thirst all that evening.

(Stainthorpe, p.24)

The process of preserving the herring is described as follows in a book of 1956:

Quite a lot happens to a herring before it becomes a kipper. It is split, gutted and washed by machinery and then it is put into a brine solution for 15–30 minutes according to the size of the herring and the taste of the customers. Next, girls impale the herrings on 'tenterhooks' which are set at intervals on 'tentersticks'. Row upon row of loaded tentersticks are placed in a brick kiln and conical heaps of wood shavings and sawdust are lighted and slowly smoke the herring… The smoking process takes upwards of six hours.

By comparison, curing is a simple process. The herrings are sprinkled with salt and put into troughs where the Scots herring-girls gut them with amazing speed... After gutting, the herrings are placed in barrels, each layer being sprinkled with fresh salt.

(Holland, 1956)

The paths of herring migration are notoriously fickle (and have enriched and impoverished cities thereby – see Mike Smylie, *Herring*, 2005). There is some recent sign that catches are improving again but little of it is headed for human consumption. For all that, good kippers can still be purchased fresh-smoked in Whitby, Craster and some other few places, or bought in shops, but they are no longer the common Northern breakfast they once were, when North Shields with its steam trawler fleet was a centre for commercial kipper smoking houses.

There was an art, too, to buying and cooking herring:

The fish-man would come round in the morning (we are only 3 miles from Newbiggin) – shouting 'Fresh harrn!' 'How much?' my Mother would ask. '6 for a shilling'... 'No, not the day'. She waited till later on, when he was on his way home, and selling the herring much more cheaply.

Fish-wives came round, calling door to door – they carried great big creels on theirs backs, full of fish, herring, mackerel, flatties...

Herring we used to bake in the oven – and eat hot or cold. You would clean the herring, split and flatten them, then roll them up and bake them in a pie dish with a little watered-down vinegar.

Or we would use a wire frame – it opens up – to toast fish esp. herring, on the fire – the wire gadget and held over the red embers of an open fire – not over flames.

(F.M., Ashington)

Others have suggested the name 'riddle' (Morpeth), more usual for a sieve, or 'toaster' (Silksworth) for this gadget. Similar, if simpler, was a 'spelder':

The device seems to have been a standard cooking item used in fishermen's homes when cooking was done on the open fire. It was either home made out of heavy gauge wire or by the local blacksmith as a sideline. They were known locally as a spelder. My grandmother had one, but it was not hinged. Fish would be cooked on one side, then turned over.

(J.C., Berwick)

A spelder

Come to think of it, the days of cod and haddock (slightly firmer and sweeter than cod?) are almost over too, and many a trawler is decommissioned (a euphemism for being cut in half and rendered useful only for scrap). Of course you can always join the local angling club and try your luck form shore or pier. If you are skilful enough to catch some fish yourself, or get them fresh as a present, here is a quick guide to how to gut (for example):

Mackerel

Cut off the head, just under the base of the gills. Slit open the length of the stomach, so that the guts come out. Cut round and dispose of the hole where the gut exits the body at the lower end. Remove the tail. Wash the insides well. Place on a baking tray, cook at Mk 5 for 15–20 minutes.

Eat hot. Or skin and bone the cooked fish and mash the meat with a fork. Cool, mix with a little salad cream (or the like) and optionally finely chopped raw onion, and use as a tasty fish pâté.

Fish pie

This uses precooked white fish, boned and skinned. (You can be economical about the type of fish you use.) Put a layer of mashed potato in the bottom of a deep pie dish; then a layer of flaked fish; then a layer of white sauce with chopped hard-boiled egg mixed in it. Then more layers of each, and top off with mashed potato. Bake in a hot oven until the potato browns on top (Mk 7, 30–40 minutes).

Note: though not exclusively North Eastern, this recipe is quite close to a Scottish dish, prepared from dry salt cod and mashed potatoes, with an egg sauce served separately (see Baxter, 1974, pp.30–31).

Fish cakes

Most economical of all, these are made of fish scraps purchased direct from the fish market. Cook them in a little lightly salted water, drain, cool, remove any skin and bones, then mix with mashed potato and some finely cut fresh parsley. Season to taste. Fry to eat now, or make a large batch and freeze for later use.

Fish can be shallow-fried, deep-fried, steamed, baked – and in the last resort eaten raw (the Japanese *sushi*) or pickled (the Swedish *rollmop*). Mind, a simple 'boiled cod, potatoes and butter beans' sounds as good as any. Undoubtedly the most popular dish, though, is 'Fish 'n' Chips'. This was an invention of the 1860s, taking advantage of the increased catch from steam trawlers, the speed of raw food supplied by railway and the popularity of seaside holidays (and day trips) that raised the demand for fast food. The fish cooks quickly in hot oil, but retains its flavour, moistness and soft texture, protected by the coating of batter. As a contrast the potato is cooked bare in the hot oil, producing a crisp exterior. The two make a perfect combination and a wonderful meal. By 1910 there were about 25,000 Fish 'n' Chip shops in Britain; 35,000 in 1927; but today under 10,000 (luckily I live within easy walking distance of two of them).

Some trawlers still make a part-time living from deep-sea fish or sea-bottom shrimps; more small craft specialise in crabs and lobsters. If you are lucky enough to get a local crab fresh, you need to scrub the shell, put it in cold water, bring to the boil and cook for some 20 minutes. A lobster is plunged (God forgive us) into boiling water, and cooks for about 15 minutes for a $1^1/2$ lb specimen and 20 minutes for $2–2^1/2$ lb oneæ but if you are new to the crustaceans, get someone with experience to help you open the shells and select the edible bits – not all of it is safe to eat.

Small shellfish are also essential to the taste of the seaside: whelks ('willocks'), cockles and mussels are traditionally served cold with a little vinegar. An American clam chowder is expensive to make in this country – but mussels might serve instead. The broth is based on a white sauce made with 'clam liquor', flavoured with a little onion, bacon, celery. Cooked clams and pre-boiled potatoes (cubed) are added in the last 15 minutes of simmering.

Basically, we suggest you eat as much of as many kinds of fish as you can while you still can. (While the boat still comes in...)

Grains

> The South has better cornland, more people, more noble cytés, and more profitable havenes.
>
> (Ranulph Higden, fourteenth century)

Grain is basic to the Western European diet; on its surplus, which can support many more than the number needed to produce it, civilisation has thrived for thousands of years. However, it did not always guarantee plenty for the farm workers: 'Poverty writes her name on raddle [sieve], pat [pot] or meal-pock [flour-sack],' sang *The British Minstrel* (Durham, 1839). In Tommy Armstrong's words:

> The miner, and his partner too, each morning have to roam,
>
> To seek for bread to feed the little hungry ones at home;
>
> The flour barrel is empty now, their true and faithful friend,
>
> Which makes the thousands wish today the strike was at an end.

For such, grain was sometimes almost the only food available: "In these parts oatmeal constitutes a principle article of food with the peasantry, not as bread but in crowdies and hasty pudding for breakfast; and sometimes for supper, eaten with butter or, more commonly, milk." (*Description of the County of Northumberland*, ca.1812) Bad harvests and high prices were especially to be feared, hence the campaigns for free trade in the first half of the nineteenth century. Today, "Oven-baked bread has now spread more or less universally ousting the thin quarter-circles or 'farls' made without yeast that once prevailed in the West [of Scotland]" (Allen, p.23)

Appropriate to the North, the grains grown would be oats and barley rather more than the more climate-wary and thus expensive wheat. Within Scotland "the basic distinction between the oatlands of the Highlander and the barley- and wheat-lands of the Lowlander is still as immutable for farmers as the climate that is its cause, but the patterns of consumption that have traditionally arisen from this have now become a great deal blurred…" (Allen, p.23) In other words, wheat can be grown in the North, but the sensible farmer and the thrifty consumer would favour the crops that best suited the land and climate.

Thus the humble barley corn prevails in the Old English *Life of St Cuthbert*, who encountered a basic farming dilemma when he tried to sow wheat on his hermitage at Inner Farne:

> …The saint had them bring seed:
>
> he wished to grow a crop   there in the wasteland
>
> if the Almighty   allowed it him
>
> that with his own footwork   he might feed himself.
>
> Thus he sowed wheat on some well-worked land   but it would not sprout
>
> not even grass   grew.
>
> Instead he asked them to bring   barley seed
>
> and though past the ideal time   he sowed it in the earth
>
> and it grew wonderfully   and well ripened.

> (trans. from Old English)

St Cuthbert might well have proceeded to make:

Barley bannocks

1 lb barley flour / 4 oz plain flour / 1 level tisp salt / 1 heaped tisp bicarb-soda / 1 heaped tisp cream of tartar / 1 pint buttermilk.

Mix; knead, roll out; bake on a griddle, both sides. (*N'd Cook Book*)

More detail is supplied in Webster's *Encyclopaedia of Domestic Cooking* (1861):

> Barley bread – This is much used in Scotland, particularly in the Highlands, also in Wales, in Devonshire and some other parts of England. The barley meal is made into bread by kneading it well with water and a little salt; it is then formed immediately either into thick or thin cakes, as may be required. When made stiff and about three quarters of an inch thick, called *Barley bannocks*, they are toasted or baked before a clear hot fire, by being placed upon the edge, and when nearly done, they require to be watched well that they may not burn. It was most likely this sort of cakes that our great Alfred was left to take care of when a goatherd and the neglect of which brought the chiding which he experienced. Very thin barley cakes called *Scons* are much used in the Highlands, particularly at breakfast; they are made by baking them quickly on an ironplate, and when well made are much relished; they are generally eaten warm with butter. (p.750)

Bread made from barley flour is dark, dry and rough in texture – for modern taste it is better mixed with other types of grain to make a more tractable dough, or used as pearl barley in broth. (Commercially, most barley today goes for animal feedstuffs, some for malting for beer.) Oats are somehow more flavoursome and would be popular as crowdy (porridge) and as the basis of oatcakes or mixed with wheat flour for bread. Wheat flour, producing 'white' bread, is common now, but would not have been so easily affordable until large quantities of hard flour were imported for bread making from Canada and the USA after 1875, halfing the price of grain. Domestic production was boosted by the scaling of land with lime (to reduce acidity). The making of bread also requires a high temperature – higher than an open wood fire can easily produce. It is not surprising that a main use of grain was as 'unleavened bread' – oatcakes and similar products, slim and easy to cook on a griddle over an open fire. So essential were these to the diet that Ferguson called Scotland 'the land o' cakes' (in his 'Leith Races').

Crowdie

Jimmy the Moudy	
Maád a great crowdy,	
Barney O'Neal	
Fand all the meal,	
<u>Oad</u> Jack Rutter	old
Sent <u>twee</u> steane o' butter,	two
The laird o' the Hot	
Boil'd it in his pot	
And big Tom o' the <u>Ho</u>'	Hall
He supped it <u>o</u>'.	all
<u>Deil</u> tak his guts, and that's o'!	Devil

(Denham Tracts, 1974, p.43)

A simple porridge is a nourishing winter dish, easily made and arguably a complete breakfast in itself. Local terms for porridge have caused some confusion: crowdy is used to describe cooked oatmeal-porridge in some areas and in others a mash of oats as a feed for fowls or as a sort of muesli for human consumption. A child holidaying north in Alnwick in the 1880s left the following telling comments on the word-use: "Oatmeal well stirred with boiling water was a 'crowdie'. I am reported to have told my granny, *'that's* what we feed our *hens* on' the first time I saw it mixed!" In Hartlepool the cooked variety turned up as "sack-porrage – hasty-pudding or porridge oatmeal mixed in boiling water and stirred on the fire till it be considerably thickened." *(Brockett)* In Co. Durham we hear of "poddish" as in the phrase "Put on the poddish-pot." *(ibid.)*

A much thinner sort of porridge, called 'skilly', was served in prisons and workhouses.

Firstly, here is:

Crowdy

Crowdy… is made by filling a basin with oatmeal, and then pouring in boiling water. A vigorous stirring action is required whilst the water us being poured; and when the two ingredients are thoroughly mixed, the 'hasty pudding' is ready.

Newcastle Monthly Chronicle (June, 1889)

Compare that with a basic recipes for preparing porridge – here after Florence White:

Porridge

2 oz medium oatmeal / 1 pt water / 1 tisp salt.

Simmer 30 mins, stir while thickening.

(Good things, p.78)

I recall my Mam used to boil it for perhaps 10 minutes and it was served with sugar and a little top of milk. If there's too much on the plate for you to manage, your Mam could always put it away atop the cupboard… leading in due course to the plea, "Come down crowdy, A'm ready for you now!"

It need not be a boring dish – "crowdy and treacle' is mentioned in the *Shields Song Book* (1826). The famous engraver Bewick talked of almost fondly of 'crowdie and milk.'" Alternative ways of serving were "oatmeal and water mixed together and used with milk butter or the fat from off the pot when beef is boiled" (*Bell MS*, Newcastle, 1815) and a luxurious "oatmeal and boiling water stirred together till thick, and then 'supped' with milk, treacle, dripping, or beer sweetened with sugar." (*Luckley*, Alnwick, 1870s). One of the simplest forms was:

Hasty pudding

$1/2$ pt boiling milk / $1/2$ teacup cold milk / 1 dessert spn flour / 1 dessert spn oatmeal / a little salt.

Mix flour, salt and oatmeal to a paste with cold milk. Add to boiling milk, return to pan; stir till thickens.

(N'd Cook Book)

Oatcakes

Oatcakes are constructed of fine oatmeal mixed with water and a little salt, and perhaps a nub of lard; lightly kneaded and patted or rolled out thin as several small or one larger round, to fit on the griddle. Note: 'cake' implies a flat round shape rather than sweetness (hence 'stotty-cake') – whereas 'loaf' implies an angular or baking-tin shape rather than a savoury base (hence 'fruit-loaf').

The oatcake is designed to be made in large batches. A preliminary cooking, almost a drying (on a griddle or the hot stones around the hearth) prepared the cakes for storage. As many as were needed at one time could then be re-toasted, for immediate use. This second cooking is said to enhance the flavour and bring a crisper texture. There was even a special frame for re-heating (for a single large oatcake).

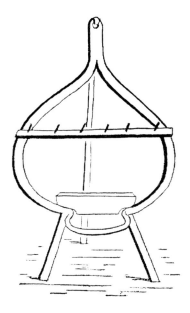

Bake-stick for reheating a large oatcake

A more detailed recipe:

Fine oatmeal: 125 gm (4 oz) / 1 tabspn fat / pinch of salt / water to mix (up to 5 tabspns)

(variants: half fine oatmeal, half wholemeal flour; or use pinhead oatmeal; add a pinch or quarter tisp. bicarbonate of soda; add a teaspoon of coarse crushed pepper).

Rub fat and salt into oatmeal and mix to a dough with the water. Roll out thin [hint: warm the oatmeal, soften the fat and use hot water to mix; roll out while dough is still warm, dusting the rolling-pin and surface with a little extra oatmeal.] Form into one large round, or several smaller rounds. Grease… Heat the griddle to a moderate heat. Test by holding your hand just above the surface when it should feel pleasantly, but not fiercely, hot. [Other authorities say, have the griddle very hot!] Bake the oatcake(s) on the hot griddle – one side only if rolled thin enough.

Cool and store, reheat or toast to eat.

A girdle cake is the name given to a slightly richer version of the oatcake, using wheat flour and eaten hot. James Horsley of Shields imagined the royal princesses (Queen Victoria's daughters) calling in on his family during their trip north in 1884. They would be warmly welcome in his terrace house…

An' wor Mally aw'm sure, just for mensefulness' syek [politeness' sake],

Wad hev gien [given] them thor teas an' a nice gordle-kyek.

A typical recipe (after Peggy Howey) might be:

8 oz flour / 2 oz currants / 1 tisp baking powder / 4 oz fat (lard, margarine, butter) / 1 tabspn sugar / milk to mix.

Rub in fat and mix with milk to a soft dough. Roll out and cut into small rounds. Bake on a hot griddle till lightly brown both sides. Split, butter and eat.

Spice-kyek and singin'-hinny

Girdle-cooking need not be limited to plain products – quite fancy items could be constructed if plenty of butter was used (in the 'singin'-hinny') or currants added (for a 'spice-cake'). These were the richest grades of girdle cake, using wheat flour rather than oatmeal, and 'singin' (so the story goes) because the butter would fizz as the cakelet cooked. They were essential to the family tea – as Joe Wilson noted in his song about a grocer's shop:

Then Sunday comes – wi' friends te tea,

When spice-kyeks florish, weel-te-de;

When corns an' raisins, floor an' lard,

Share i' the hoosewife's kind regard

['Corns' here surely means seeds; 'spice' refers to currants usually, not the modern range of powdered flavourings.]

Wilson also records the process from the consumer's point of view:

So wor Mally myed up, on the Seturday neet,

Bowt spice loaf an' fancy kyecks, iverything sweet,

An' wi jellies an' marmilades really myed free,

Fairly meant te luck decent when frinds com te tea.

So on Sunday, when dinner was ower that day,

Like a gud handy hoosewife she clear'd things away,

An' wor new tyeble-cloth, just as white as cud be,

Had a real grand invitin appearance for tea.

The cups wes a' set, an' the wigs [currant tea-cakes] nice an' het

Wes butter'd, then cut up se neat be me pet,

An' the bairn, wiv a lump iv its hand, full o' glee,

Seem'd te knaw thor wes sumbody cummin te tea…

Moving forward to the 1930s, the important role of Sunday teatime is also recorded by Charles Trelogan of New Herrington, near Sunderland:

Sunday for tea was the day for socialising or family gatherings. When everyone wore their best and the best china was brought out and when, depending on circumstances, the children of the hosts were given a small gift of money. The time of the last bus, on a Sunday limited service, was very important. Children were seated first and inevitably they rushed to finish the sandwiches to get first choice of the cream cakes. Cream horns were the favourites.

Not cream cakes but singin'-hinnies were the staple of an earlier tea-time. Brockett's *Dictionary* noted: "singin'-hinnie or stinging-hinny" – a rich kneaded cake; indispensable in a pitman's family.

Singin'-hinny

A typical recipe for a singin'-hinny follows, from a newscutting of 1937:

8 oz flour / $^1/_2$ pint milk/ $^1/_2$ tispn baking powder / $^1/_4$ tispn salt / $^1/_2$ lb lard or butter rubbed in / 3 oz currants / 4 oz castor sugar / large pinch powdered cinnamon.

Mix to dough with $^3/_4$ pint milk and water, roll out to $^1/_4$ inch thick on floured board, cut in rounds about 3 inch diameter. Bake for about 20 minutes on a hot greased girdle and when cooked, smear a little fresh butter and dust a little castor sugar on top of each.

Variants:

Include the use of currants, sultanas and/or raisins, and half a grated lemon rind. Proportion of flour to shortening 3:2, sometimes only 2:1. Or use half lard, half butter. Small amounts of baking powder, baking soda and/or cream of tartar – combined with sour cream or milk. (The use of sour milk is not strictly recommended since a few fatalities in the DIY kitchen during World War 2.)

The use of an egg as well as milk.

A recipe based on about a pound of flour (2$^1/_2$ cups) recommended you should: "Divide dough into 24 balls.

Flatten to round cakes. Bake on a greased cooking sheet in a preheated oven 425°F for about 12–15 minutes or until golden brown." (But of course a griddle would do it better!)

According to Florence White (1932, pp.83–84), "roll to ¹/₄ inch thick, bake on greased griddle, both sides, 10–15 mins, then first side again for luck – eat hot, cut into pieces, split and buttered".

Somewhere in between a singin'-hinny and a crumpet was the pikelet; the following recipe is from Florence White:

Pikelets

8 oz flour / ¹/₂ tisp salt / 2 tisp castor sugar / 1 tisp cream of tartar / ¹/₂ tisp carbonate of soda / 1 egg / ¹/₄ pt milk / ¹/₄ pt water.

Assemble dry ingredients, add egg yolk only, make a batter with milk, etc., fold in whisked egg white.

Bake on hot greased griddle – pour on batter in tabspns. Brown one side, then brown tuther.

It would be hard to take leave of tea-time without a little more information on the beverage itself. Although there may have been miners who could not start their shift until carried, limp, on their comrades' shoulders to the nearest Starbuck's for a double shot of expresso coffee, the majority of them and us have operated on tea. The reduction of tax in 1784 and the promotion of tea-growing in India in the 1840s made it inevitable that tea would become the popular drink of refreshment (as opposed to beer, the drink of entertainment). A rounded earthenware teapot gave the tea-leaves room to mash or mask (Anglo-Saxon and Viking respectively) before 'teeming out' into the tea-cup.

Curiously it was an American tea-merchant, Thomas Sullivan, who altered all this by unwittingly inventing the tea-bag in 1908. He sent samples out in silk pouches, intending the pouches to be opened and the tea used loose as normal. His customers, puzzled by this new form of packaging, put the whole bag into the pot, and were impressed by the convenience of this new system. By the 1920s, tea-bags were in commercial production in the USA, silk being replaced by gauze and eventually paper. This new solution to making a cuppa became popular in the UK in the 1960s; today 85% of our tea is brewed this way. It has led to redundancy for the tea-pot and the tea-cup; it is simpler to put a single tea-bag into a single mug (or 'pot' in miners' speech) and pour on boiling water. It certainly saves time and labour; the result is as good as, some would say better than ever before.

Sugar

Where did the Scots end up who were captured in battle by the English from the seventeenth century on? In the West Indies, to serve as labourers on the sugar cane estates. What were they fed on? Cured herring, exported from the UK. This neat if harsh circle of people and food-stuffs underlines the importance of sugar in the diet and economy in early modern times, not least to a European City of Culture like Liverpool.

Sugar played a remarkably versatile role, as flavouring in tea, coffee, an ingredient in sweet puddings, an addition to breakfast cereals, etc.; as a preservative, in fruit jams, marmalades and fruit 'cheeses'; as a source of energy and entertainment for bairns as boiled sweets, toffee and fairground candy-floss; and as a source of alcohol in homemade wines.

Caramel toffee (claggum)

6 oz butter / 6 oz sugar / 8 oz syrup / 1 tin condensed milk.

Melt butter and sugar, then add syrup, let these come to boil, then add milk. It must be constantly stirred or it will burn. Boil until thick and put into greased tin to set.

(Shildon recipe book, ca. 1935)

'Sugarless' toffee   *(Kathleen Teward, Teesdale)*

1 tin sweetened condensed milk / 2 oz margarine / 2 tabspns golden syrup / a little vanilla essence.

Combine all ingredients and bring to the boil. Boil for 15 minutes; pour into greased tin and allow to cool.

Taffle apple   *(Florence Merihein, Ashington)*

16 oz demerara sugar; 8 oz butter or margarine; 1 large tabspn golden syrup; a tabspn malt vinegar.

Place butter and sugar in a saucepan, stir and bring to boil. Add syrup and vinegar; boil for about 20 minutes or until a small amount dropped in cup of cold water turns hard. Pour toffee into a greased flat tin to set, or make toffee apples using eating apples and some narrow pieces of wood (lollipop sticks would do). Push stick into apple where stalk was then dip into the hot toffee to coat; let stand on greased paper sheet or greaseproof paper to set.

Boiled sweets are mentioned honourably in the early nineteenth century, when 'Black Bullets' were manufactured in memorial to the round shot that killed Nelson. Workers at Welch's Sweets recalled:

> Black mints were very popular in those days [decade after 1945], what we would now call 'black bullets'. We used to sell them not only in England but more or less all over the Empire. They particularly liked them in Jamaica because they liked to put them in a bottle of coke…

(Armstrong & White, 1997, p.37)

In 1845 there is a mention of "gilded spice-babies and sticks of barley sugar" (Newc Cen Lib, L042, vol.12, p.8). Most children have 'a sweet tooth' and many a working miner appreciated a sweet to keep his throat moist down the mine. Fortunately several major sweet manufacturers were located in the North East: including Welch's of North Tyneside (a family firm that goes back to 1919) and Horner's of Chester-le-Street (manufacturers of 'Dainty Dinah' toffees) which shut down in 1960. Yet fantastic shapes and colours of sweets remain a feature of many a small shop, within our easy reach. Here is a list of sweets from the 1920s by A. B. Ward, set down in one of Jean Crocker's dialect workshops:

Baccy – fine shredded coconut covered with chocolate powder.
Black bullets – black mints.
Bullseyes – which changed colour as one sucked them.
Crystal clear fishes – red, yellow and white.
Dolly mixtures – small candy shapes.
Lucky tyetties [potatoes] – type of marzipan or paste containing lucky charms.
Pit props – thick logs of coconut candy.
Seaside mixtures – small candies looking like sea shells and pebbles.
Sherbert dabs – a dab of toffee on a stick which you licked and dabbed in your sherbert.
Sherbert fountains – where you sucked the sherbert through a tube of liquorice.
Sweethearts – heart shaped candies.
Tyne mints – orange coloured strong mints.

(Accent on the North East: Dialect jottings, 1983)

Plus:

Jelly babies, liquorice telephones, liquorice bootlaces, liquorice pipes, liquorice blow balls, aniseed balls and gob stoppers, acid, pear or pineapple drops, etc.

There was also a special role for Spearmint Bouncers:

When summer changed to autumn on Saturday afternoons the Hall Road Boys would walk down to the cinema in Hebburn old town. On arrival at the cinema we bought twopenny tickets for the upstairs seats (downstairs seats cost a penny). Noise prevailed everywhere. We never saw adults in that auditorium, except one attendant and the long suffering manager. Our Boys always sat on an elevated pocket of seats above the circle and in the left hand pocket, not the right hand one.

If ever the mistake was made by the management of putting on a love film, the normal pandemonium was raised to cries of outrage. Feet were stamped all around the hall and from our group came the chant, "We want Hoot". The 'Hoot' we cried for was Hoot Gibson our favourite cowboy hero.

At last Mr Dawe, the manager, would come out onto the stage in front of the screen still showing the Romance film. He then lifted both hands above his head and implored us for silence, but this was the moment we had been waiting for and with one accord we took from our pockets handfuls of spearmint bouncers and hurled them at Mr Dawe on the stage. Spearmint bouncers were small, round, white sweets which when eaten tasted of spearmint. The small white balls landed in an avalanche on the stage. Mr Dawe would then turn, lower his head and walk quickly off the stage. Soon afterwards the romance film came to an abrupt ending and the title of a film starring Hoot Gibson was flashed on the screen. The bedlam now changed to cheers, then within seconds order was restored as Hoot could be seen leaping from an upstairs window onto the back of his horse. Those Saturday afternoon matinées meant a lot to us all.

(Terry Cummins)

In the adult world, sugar was essential in preserving fresh fruits, which decayed within a few days of picking. Strawberries, raspberries, blackberries are typical fruits you were likely to encounter as jam – in World War One, schoolchildren were enlisted for special blackberry picking days, to maximise the use of local resources. (Rosehips were also collected this way.) On the higher moorlands, wild bilberries are a delicious free fruit.

Commercially, the summer involved a round of picking, moving through gooseberries, red currants, black currants, raspberries to plums, pears and apples – most was sold in bulk to jam factories, some prime fruit ending up in markets and shops. Alas, commercial fruit growing in the region largely ended during World War 2. (Hartley, 1972, p.95)

Gooseberries ('grozers' in Northumberland, 'goosegogs' in Co. Durham) were clearly appreciated, and newspapers in the 1820s and 1830s regularly report end-of-summer gooseberry shows and flower contests. John Bell notes a 'grozer smasher' in the 1810s – 'a small standing pye made of gooseberries.' For the following recipe, fruit is ideally collected from wayside bushes in the higher land of west Co. Durham or the Tyne Valley:

Wild gooseberry jam

2 lbs goosegogs / 1 pt water / 2$^{1}/_{2}$ lbs sugar.

Collect 2 lbs gooseberries – preferably the small, reddish-tinged type that grows wild at altitude; top and tail; place in a pan with approx 1 pt water and simmer until soft but retaining shape. Add sugar, stir in, bring back to boil and continue boiling and stirring until the temperature reaches 105°C (using a cooking thermometer) or until large, slow, richly-plopping bubbles form (approx. 15 minutes). Bottle.

(W.L.)

It is a short step from jam-making to wine-making. The same sort of fruits are involved, e.g. blackberries, blackcurrants, cherries, plus a range of alternative local ingredients like elderflowers, elderberries, coltsfoot flowers and even parsnips (which make a wonderful scented wine). Milestones in the history of homemade wine are the heavy duties levied on imported alcohol during the French Wars of 1793–1815 and the abolition of duties levied on the import of sugar in 1874. If you could not afford the whiskey smuggled from Scotland, the gin smuggled from Holland or the brandy smuggled from France, then DIY wine was a very practical solution.

In the mining towns, beer was the standard drink, which is quick to brew, but requires some special ingredients and processing. The proper basis of beer is the malt liquor derived from steeping barley that has been germinated and roasted. Any sizeable household would brew its own beer, much as it would bake its own bread. (The processes had been linked together since Ancient Egyptian times.) Hops are often said to have been first introduced from Holland in the fifteenth century. However, an excavation of the tenth century 'Graveney Boat' in Kent (*BAR* 53, 1978) revealed a cargo of hops being brought in from the Rhineland. Besides, the hop plant is probably native to this country – at least in the warmer South; also evidence of hops occurs in excavations of Viking York.

The antiquarian William Stukeley, on a journey north in 1725, remarked of the area around Newcastle:

> In some parts of this country, the ordinary people make a good sort of ale called *hather*, that is, ling ale, by boiling the tips of the Hather plant to a wort… and ferment it.
>
> (*Itinerarium curiosum*, vol.2 p.64)

Whilst John Bailey mentions treacle beer (also called 'treacle wow') in use in Co. Durham in 1810.

However, with the concentration of population in towns and cities in the nineteenth century and the increasing role of Newcastle as a centre of entertainment, the beer was likelier supplied by a commercial brewery and found a ready market, not only in the cities but in the colliery settlements with their working men's clubs and thirsty miners – this was social drinking on a scale well beyond the local household's capacity to brew. Not the first, but arguably the most famous of these commercials beers is Newcastle Brown, brewed from 1927 – commercial brewing can claim to date back to 1779 in Newcastle.

Incidentally, there seems little to choose between the terms 'yal' (ale) and 'beer'. The Old English word for barley was 'bere', but 'byggja' in Old Norse – hence the Bigg Market in Newcastle.

Strong drink has always been associated with celebrations. Let the last word go to Thomas Wilson, who, after a road planning decision in his favour back in 1826, promised:

> How 'way Dicky, how 'way hinney,
> There's the tooting o' the horn,
> If it cost a gowden ginney
> Thou's be soak'd wi' barley corn…

Coda

If the recipes for cooking on an open fire seem at times plain and even uninspiring, that is surely in contrast to current technicolour food opportunities. In fact, the griddle could cook a range of foods from thin steaks to fillets of fish; its work today is continued by the domestic frying-pan and the more commercial hot-plate that cooks many a bacon and egg breakfast in local cafés. The old-style open fire was well suited to roasting on a spit, and something of that pleasure of direct cooking draws us to the BBQ perhaps. The magic of toast browned at an open fire seemed an adventure unequalled. Combined with griddle and kale-pot the open hearth was surprisingly versatile and enduring. Indeed, 'Today the Northerner still prefers to boil where the Southerner roasts or grills: the cooking-pot, as always, resisting the advance of the oven.' (Allen, 1968, p.23)

Part two – the era of th' yuven

... the area, one might say, is Scotland plus the oven.

(Allen, 1968, p.173)

Introducing th' yuven

The oven was originally a separate cooking facility from the domestic hearth, dedicated to the production of bread. Bread needs a fiercer heat than an open wood fire easily affords and a surrounding rather than a uni-directional heat source. (Initial high heat is needed to kill the yeast, halt the rising process and 'set' the texture of the loaf; sustained surrounding heat ensures the loaf is cooked through.) The bread oven would therefore be a structure on its own, ideally in a separate 'bakehouse', safely detached from the living quarters. Such an oven, of the Viking period, is believed to have been found in a 'kitchen block' in the remains of a farm excavated at Ribblehead.

In a wooden building, such an oven would need to be central; in a stone building, it could be more conveniently built into the wall. From its typically domed shape it has become known as a 'beehive' oven and in old stone farmhouses in the North East examples are found athwart the outside wall, half-in, half-out of the kitchen, showing as a mounded bulge at the exterior. The size would depend on the household to be served and in turn would influence the material used: it could be built of stone or brick (i.e. any available fire-resisting/heat-retaining material) – and sealed with clay or turf. An oven itself of clay is not impossible: the *OED*, under 'oven', notes in Scotland, 1513, a payment 'to the baxtaris of the greit schip for clay to make an une in the greit schip.'

Inside the oven a fire would be lit, using brushwood and small off-cuts rather than logs or large branches – the aim being a quick and fierce heat. Once the oven was truly hot, the remnants of the fire would be raked and brushed out – swiftly, to avoid heat-loss. Any flue would be closed off next. Risen loaves were then placed on the floor of the hot oven with a wooden paddle (much as used by professional bakers to this day) and the front opening sealed off. The loaves were left to cook in the residual heat from the oven walls.

For those for whom an oven was not practicable, an economic alternative was a small 'portable' version (e.g. the 'cloam oven' of Devon) – an earthenware vessel that could be super-heated in an open domestic fire, to take a single loaf to bake. These probably did not differ much from the individual-loaf size earthenware 'ovens' used in olden Roman households. Not that building a proper beehive oven took that much trouble to build. Here is how it is done (courtesy of Aoife Finn's website):

> We used field stone from a local stone wall… which is relatively flat and somewhat uniformly shaped. It was thus easy to arrange the stone into shapes that would work well as our round oven. On advice from another 'oven expert', we used a 14" clay flower pot as the top half of the oven rather than stone. In retrospect, the stone corbelled nicely and we will probably use all stone next year. The oven building process, all in all, took about three hours. While some folks use a huge layer of clay or mud as insulation, this was not available to us. Instead we used the sod we cut from the fire pits. As an insulator it worked quite well so long as we ensured that the chinks were all filled in with dirt between the stone (dirt excavated from the fire pits and the oven floor). A large stone was found to use as a hearthstone and this proved to be the perfect touch, ensuring our success.

How to fire and use an earthen oven:

> Use kindling to start a small fire inside the oven. Chop firewood into slim, short pieces and use these to build a quick, hot fire. Keep this fire going fairly strong – fire shooting out the top hole (if you have one) is appropriate so long as you do not set the camp on fire! We pre-heated the oven for the length of time it took the bread to go through two risings on a chilly day (about three hours). By this time we judged it had stored enough heat to bake our bread. The fire was shovelled out and the ashes swept out quickly and the loaves were placed inside. The oven was sealed with a rock door that had also been pre-heated (use thick leather gloves to handle large, hot rocks!). The bread baked in the expected amount of time. The oven had to go through another brief firing in order to bake a second batch.
>
> Why bother? I hypothesized that when the oven used was different from our modern ovens, the end product would be different from bread baked in a modern oven. I was absolutely correct and don't mind if I seem silly when I brag about it. You see, bread baked in such a manner has a rougher crust and retains some of the flavour of the wood smoke. Nothing I can describe to you can impart the experience of a wholemeal loaf baked with fruitwood or maplewood smoke. You simply must experience it some time in your life!

Other experimenters add some useful details: it might take two to four hours to achieve the right heat (375–400°F). If coal is the fuel, any remaining burning coals can be returned to the kitchen's open fire, ashes to a compartment under the oven called the ash box. One method of checking the right heat was to scatter a little flour on the oven floor and note how quickly it browned.

An outdoor oven is clearly safer, but given the vagaries of the weather, not so practical as a bread oven in the main kitchen area, either the beehive sort mentioned above or metal casing inserted in a rectangular or round cavity in the wall. At Mr Tod's house, according to Beatrix Potter, "The light showed a little door in a wall beside the kitchen fireplace – a little iron door belonging to a brick oven, of that old-fashioned sort that used to be heated with faggots of wood". These built-in wall-ovens became a not uncommon feature of the farmhouse kitchen during the eighteenth century, but still required their own dedicated source of heat, i.e. were not directly heated by the main kitchen fire. That the oven and open fire were in proximity was a matter of convenience: both were needed in the kitchen where food was prepared, both needed to be in a fire-proof part of the house; both needed a common space to store and dry fuel.

Baking bread was a relatively complex process, needing both a special oven and a good deal of time to prepare. It was the opposite of a quickly-made convenience food. Its production would only really be justified at household level plus, with a special baking once (or more) a week. In the mining era, a communal bread-oven might serve a terrace row of houses; in the cities, a commercial baker might offer the use of his oven (for a small fee). A description of baking on this scale is provided in Websters' *Encyclopaedia of Domestic Cooking* (1861, p.761):

The ovens employed by bakers and likewise in general use by families in the country, where sometimes a considerable quantity of bread is prepared, are built of bricks.

The common brick oven is of a circular or oval plan and is arched over with good sound bricks, the bottom being laid with flat tiles, closely joined... The oven is heated by wood, introduced by the door, laid upon the floor and kindled. When the bricks are sufficiently hot the fire is withdrawn and the ashes carefully swept out, when the bread is introduced. While the wood is burning, the smoke goes through the flue; but when the bread is put in, the inner door (to the flue) is closed and likewise the outer, to keep in the heat. The bread is baked merely by the heat of the brickwork and when it has remained a sufficient time, the doors are opened, and the baked bread is taken out.

Coal is now very generally employed by bakers in towns for heating the oven instead of wood and is found to answer perfectly, at less expense.

The appeal of bread

Despite the effort involved, bread is (in Western terms) a well-attested historic item of diet, of demonstrable popularity. The Old English word *bread* refers to texture, the 'crumb': compare Old English *bio-bread* (literally 'bee-bread') for honeycomb. *Hlaf* for loaf is there in Old English, and the *hlaford* or lord was the bread-provider, the *hlafdige* or lady, the bread-preparer.

The preference for bread over, say, oatcake, given the complexity of preparing and baking bread, needs some explanation. The aerated texture makes it easier and more agreeable to chew; the resilience combined with texture makes it ideal for sopping up the liquid of a stew. When St Cuthbert was stranded in the wilds without food, a miraculous meal appeared of 'wearm hlaf mid his syfling' (a warm loaf with its accompaniment; *sufel* in Old English can apply to cheese, meat, apples...) – the implication being that many food stuffs were simply regarded as what you ate with bread. Then there is the flavour – flour modified by the action of yeast undergoes complex organic changes including the production of alcohol (driven off during the baking), the enhancement of proteins and the partial breaking down of carbohydrates. Arguably, the modified and expanded form of grain available in cooked bread is more digestible than its unleavened form in oatcakes.

Wheat, barley and oats were all grown in the North, but in a region where oats were more readily and cheaply available than wheat, the humble oatcake had some clear advantages. They were simpler to make, lasted better than bread, and were more portable and practical. Thus when the piper's son sets off on a journey in George MacDonald's novel *The Marquis of Lossie*, he took 'some provisions for the voyage, consisting chiefly of oatcakes.' (ch.8) They were the Northern land-based equivalent of the ship's biscuit. If oatmeal were the ingredient most readily at hand, an oatcake might well seem better value than troubling over an oatmeal loaf or expending money on wheaten flour, and a farmer might think twice before fitting an oven in a cottage to be used by temporary farmhands.

The situation is now reversed. Bread is widely and cheaply available, ready-cooked and fortified with vitamins and protein, whereas the crunchy oatcake is a connoisseur item. This is partly accounted for by the suitability of bread for mass production, but also its adaptability for portable snacks. The sandwich has dominated our concept of quick food for over two centuries and was the basis of a pitman's *bait*.

The development that made the pitman's sandwich a reality during the course of the nineteenth century was...

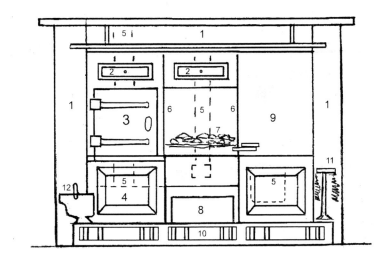

Diagram of kitchen range (drawn by Charles Trelogan)

Key:

1. Stone surround, with brass shelf below top.
2. Removable panels for cleaning; linked to plate ends on rod to control heat.
3. Hinged oven door with shelf in front.
4. Space below oven that could be fed from fire to increase oven heat.
5. Flues conducting hot air from fire.
6. Metal sheets forming fire surround.
7. Raised shelf at back with reserve of coal.
8. Ash box.
9. Small hot water cistern accessible by tap or ladle.
10. Concrete or stone hearth with metal fender.
11. A 'tidy' comprising poker, rake and tongs.
12. Coal scuttle.

The kitchen range

The strong heat produced by burning coal made it suitable for virtually every cooking process, including baking bread and roasting meat. Perhaps it was inevitable that sooner or later someone would combine the standard kitchen open coal fire and the bread oven. The key proved to be the use of cast iron…

The purpose-built kitchen range was a complete unit in iron that incorporated open coal fire and oven(s). In manufacture from about 1800 onward, in older properties the whole fitted neatly inside a large open fireplace, while "after about 1850, new working-class homes were usually fitted with ranges that had at least a small oven." (Eveleigh, 1982, p.21) This coincided usefully with the repeal of the Corn Laws, on the eve of a shift in grain preferences: "(a) dramatic fall in price of wheat in the 1880s led to a decline in the eating of oat and barley bread." (Tibbott, 1982, p.6)

Essentially the range was a coal fire in a metal grate with metal ovens on one or both sides. The simplest 'combination grate' was an open fire with trivets and one oven at the left. With two ovens, one would serve for baking, the other for heating water for the miner's bath and other domestic chores. The boiler would be topped up from above and drawn off via a tap low down. Later on, there might also be a back boiler to heat water for pipes to local taps.

A modification of this was the closed kitchen range or 'kitchener', in which the fire was enclosed within the range and an iron hob ran continuously across the top of ovens and fire: "The typical kitchener consisted of two ovens, one each side of the grate and a boiler behind, each heated by a separate flue." (Eveleigh, 1983, p.27)

From 1929 on, the Swedish 'Aga' was available in this country, originally designed to burn coke, but now available for a range of fuels: gas, electricity and oil. They remain necessary in many a farm house.

The advantage of the kitchen range was that the fire served as the source of heat for multiple uses and in particular enabled an effective, ready-to-use oven, considerably increasing the scope of the cook's repertoire. By combining oven and hob (or oven and open fire), meat and vegetables could be cooked separately to form one course, while a second sweet course was also cooking – a decided benefit to the menu.

The oven would be heated partly by proximity to the fire but additionally and more importantly by flues that conducted hot air from the fire beside it around the outside of the oven chamber, ensuring that a general all-round heat was maintained in the oven. Extra heat could be raised by banking hot coals against the oven side; sometimes burning coal or hot ash could be raked sideways to a small chamber below the oven, to ensure maximum heat in the oven itself. Inside the oven would be some three sets of side guides for shelves of plate iron that let you set one or more items to cook at different levels. A smaller oven for slow cooking, warming plates or keeping food hot might be fitted in above or below the main oven. In front of the oven and/or the fire, a useful metal shelf or fender gave you somewhere to rest hot cooking utensils and a convenient stand for rising bread dough. Swivelling trivets could let you position (and remove) a kettle or pot over the heat, in the case of a central open fire. (Alternately, a 'bar' could be hooked over the front of the fire grate to support a kettle or the like.)

> The fire had fire-bars in front, and a shelf at back – onto that shelf reserve coal could be placed, to be pulled forward onto the fire as needed with a coal rake [long metal shaft with small foot at right angles at end]. A small stand could be hooked onto the fire-bars, where pans rested to keep warm. The fire was kept in 24 hours a day.
>
> (E.J., Trimdon)

A variant on the rectangular oven was a circular oven – the 'Newcastle round oven' – a "cast-iron oven, with two shelves and brass fall handle in oven door." (Carron, Catalogue, 1908, still on offer in their 1933 catalogue.) The cylinder shape may have aided an even distribution of hot air around the outside. It also served as an economical alternative to large ranges, as 'Newcastle' ovens came in a variety of sizes and could be bought as separate units, perhaps to be fitted into the wall next to an existing open fire.

Newcastle round oven

The kitchen range was practical, time-consuming and (after a fashion) decorative. After each major cooking spree, the fire itself and the flues to the oven would have to be cleared of soot, clinker and ash. In the case of really stubborn accumulations…

> …tongs, my mother used them for blasting the oven out with a bit powder. The men must have fetched it home. She would wrap it round the bit powder in a lot of paper, and get hold of it with the tongs, and shove it down the oven and it went 'pft'. She would get some nice baking done after that, it must have been shot powder from the pit."
>
> (Polly Lee, via Beamish)

Next, the show metalwork on the front of the oven would be burnished or worked over with black-lead, producing a pleasing muted glow. The fire itself could be kept in overnight, banked up with small-coal (also called slack, dolly-muck, duff, etc.). Thus: 'At night we merely banked them up and then "blazed" them up again the next morning ready for the fray.'

(Stainthorpe, p.24)

The range was something of a multi-purpose convenience – the practical and decorative centre of the kitchen...

The range was a cooker set in large 'fireplace', i.e. cement frame. In front would be a fender, about 1 foot high, made of steel. One could stand on the fender to reach the mantlepiece above – where clock, china dogs, brass candlesticks, etc. were grouped.

There would be a rope or brass line under mantlepiece for drying clothes. (This could also be done in back lane, but then would have to be taken down if coal cart or midden cart came.)

In centre of opening was the fire grate proper – lifted up from floor level – underneath was a space for ashes – if you were lucky you could get local blacksmith to make an ash pan or box to catch ashes and make cleaning easier.

(E.J., Trimdon)

The now fashionable china dogs and two large ornaments and brass candlesticks adorned the mantle, a brass line ran underneath for drying clothes and the rest was enlivened by a high steel fender and massive fire irons. Pokers had to be long in those days, for fireplaces were deep set and often took five buckets of coals. A cracket always stood near the fire and a rocking chair. Fridays were nightmare days when all brass and steel had to be cleaned and placed on the round table until the Saturday.

(J.T., Trimdon)

Monday was washing day, so a batch of cooking might wait till Thursday. On a baking day, a hot fire was needed, but there was no simple regulo control to give a guide to the oven temperature. "Cooking then was not an exact science – it was a matter of experience – you could get some idea by feeling the handle on the oven..." (M.R.) Or by putting you arm in the oven. Or:

I have an old Be-Ro cookery book (everybody learned to bake form the Be-Ro book) and among the hints to the housewife for testing an oven temperature was this:

1. If a sheet of writing paper burns when put in, the oven is too hot.

2. If the paper becomes dark brown, the oven is suitable for pastry and scones.

3. If light brown, it does for buns and cakes (small).

4. I dark yellow, for cakes.

5. If light yellow, for biscuits.

The temperature may be easily reduced by placing a bowl of water in it.

(J.O., Forest Hall)

For a beginner, therefore, using a range could be something of a test:

Sally made a pudden
Shoo made it ower sweet;
Shoo dursn't stick a knife in't
Till Jack cam home at neet.

John, wilta have a bit like?
Don't say nay,
For last Monday mornin'
Was aar weddin'-day.

(Moorman, 1916)

The elaborate procedure of the kitchen range meant that when the fire was built-up and the oven heated thoroughly for a batch of cooking, maximum use was made of the time (as related to me by Margaret Reed of Seaham). A spare piece of dough could be placed on a metal sheet in the oven to cook while the oven heated up and while the loaves proper underwent their final rising in tins – this would make a flat, round loaf known variously as stotty-cake or new cake.

Bread needed maximum oven heat – so went in when the oven was at its hottest.

Afterwards, teacakes could be cooked, then pastry and when the oven was a little cooler still, cakes could be put in (chocolate cake, orange cake, walnut cake, rice cake…). In its final cooling, a delicious rice pudding could still be cooked, taking 3–4 hours. (A Christmas cake was best cooked overnight as the fire died slowly down – a footnote from Framwellgate.) As a good example of slow cooking, we cite the following:

Fluffin *(a Christmas dish)*

1 oz rice / 1 oz sugar / 1 pt milk / a little grated nutmeg /some brandy.

This is a variant on rice pudding, using barley. Bring barley to the boil in milk; add sugar and nutmeg to taste and a drop or two of brandy. Place in a pudding dish in the oven and let cook slowly until milk is absorbed.

Butter beans

$^1/_2$ lb butter beans / 2 rashers bacon / 1 onion / 2 tomatoes / pint of stock / 2 dessert spns golden syrup.

Soak dry butterbeans overnight and drain, or drain and wash tinned butter beans; cut up and lightly fry bacon, onion, tomato; place all, with stock, in an oven dish in a slow/medium oven for 30–40 minutes; add golden syrup 10 minutes before the end. Serve with toast.

The kitchen routine

All this made optimum use of the oven, so that not every day would have to be a 'baking day', indeed trays of buns or cakes might only need to be made once a week. In that case, there was still a role for the oatcake on a griddle to supplement the bread supply during the week: "Heating the large oven would be confined to one specific day in every week and subsequently the family's supply of bread and cakes would be augmented by that which could be baked over the open fire." (Tibbott, p.22–3)

The open fire was still a major cooking opportunity and could be used for cook-pot, kettle, frying-pan or girdle (griddle). If the hob was continuous above the fire, that would serve as the cooking surface and explains why pots and pans now have flat bottoms. The round bottomed kale-pot was replaced by the saucepan, while a straight-sided, flat-bottomed cooking vessel, made from sheet metal, with a separate lid, but no side handle, has become known as a kettle.

Most meals would be eaten in the kitchen. Breakfast for better-fed children in the 1920s might be a cup of cocoa (made with half milk, half water), toast or a boiled egg sandwich, or porridge in winter. Bread spread with butter and sugar was a popular (and high energy) food.

> And every house had a toasting fork hanging by the side of the fireplace. And we used to get it, me mother used to cut it pretty thick, about three quarters of an inch thick, a nice slice off the beautiful home made bread, and hold it in front of the fire there. And then you could, you'd get dripping or mebbies margarine on it again for your, for

your breakfast. And, by, that dripping used to be lovely on the hot bread because it used to melt in, and it wasn't half very very tasty. But that was what we used to get. We always got our breakfast at home and then we used to go to school for dinner, get your tea at home and then go up and get your cocoa, cocoa every night.

George Patterson (Beamish, 2004/61)

For the working man there was seldom time for a cooked breakfast. He might have some porridge or a cup of tea; his bait for work would be left ready – sandwiches in a tin and a tin bottle with a cork for his tea (black and sugared). The can of cold tea might be reheated over a candle down the pit. The miner would appreciate meat, cheese or jam in his sandwich or stotty; or he might make do with sugar or treacle. In Wheatley Hill, they claim that Christmas cake – with cheese – was used to make special sandwiches in the New Year. Some miners would take a small pot of jam down with them as they reckoned it helped clear the throat of dust. The main meal of the day would be timed to suit the end of the miner's shift – not easy if several members of the same family worked different shifts!

In our mining family, Dad went to work about 2 am, roused by the pit buzzer – a slice of bread and jam would be left for him for his breakfast, and a kettle on the bar, to make a cup of tea. There would be a tin bottle of water and some jam sandwiches for him to take to work (he loved fig and lemon jam!). Us kids would be up by 7.45 am for school; Dad would be back from the pit about 10.45 am, his dinner would be ready for 11 am; then we would be home from school for our dinner at 12.15 pm; our tea would be 4 pm. Our big brother also worked at the pit – but he would want his dinner at 5.30 pm. Only on a Saturday and Sunday would our meals coincide!

(F.M., Ashington)

Keith's mother never seemed to sleep. With four sons and a husband, all on shift work, no matter what the time of day or night that they returned home, there was always a freshly cooked hot meal waiting for them.

In the oven, at the side of the coal fire, she had a stockpot that simmered 24 hours a day. On a cold winter's night it would be lovely to go to Keith's house. His mother would ladle out beautiful steaming bowls of this wonderful tasting stew. With slices of her freshly baked yeasty bread, it was a meal fit for princes of the realm.

(T. M.)

Such a domestic routine was a far from idyllic existence; it was time-consuming, but workable and a real improvement over the possibilities of open fire alone. The terrace house, with its rear kitchen, outshot scullery with a set-pot for washing clothes, yard to dry clothes and an outdoor coal-shed and netty has long been overtaken by a more convenient (time-saving) way of life; yet its design as a building was well thought out and the sturdy stone or brick terrace house may yet outlive many a modern executive 'bumlor-box' (matchbox to carry a bee in!), intended to last about as long as the mortgage does.

The kitchen range or 'black range' also had a social function and an open coal fire can be as entertaining (or more so) than a television:

> A big coal fire dominated every miner's house. To its right, as in ours, stood the oven and to the left a big 'belly' boiler. This fed our bath but many people still had to fill their tin bath by hand, using a tin pot. The fire served not only to heat the room, albeit inefficiently and somewhat dustily, but also as a focal point for the family. Greeting every visitor was an imposing array of fire irons, poker, coal rake and blazer, together with a big brass fender. Unfortunately, the fire also produced a regular supply of ashes which had to be cleared out every day. Women had to clean and polish the fireplace regularly and the producers of black lead must have made their fortune in the North East.
>
> (Stainthorpe, pp.23–24, re Shotton Colliery)

The kitchen range was essential to the terrace house way of life and continued in use longer in mining villages than elsewhere. In 1968 it was noted that "over 90% of homes [in the North] still rely on solid fuel as their principal source of heating" and "more cookers here are still run on solid fuel." (Allen, p.174, p.155) They are popular again as status items; but for their use, you would do well to go and observe the skills in practice at Beamish Museum.

Stotties and fadges

There is some speculation (argument) over the difference between a stottie and a fadge. Originally they are different words for a round loaf: 'fadge' reflecting the dialect word 'fad' (for a bundle of anything) and the preferred term north of the Tyne; 'stottie' meaning 'bouncy' (i.e. yeast-based) has become the standard term south of the Tyne. It is also said that the fadge is of fuller shape, being risen twice whereas as a stottie rises but once and therefore is flatter. The stottie may also achieve its flatness by having an indent made in the centre of the risen stottie with a thumb, and by being turned during cooking. (I will be happy to adjudge these subtleties, when I can find a shop that sells fadges and stotties side by side.) To understand their basically flat, circular shape properly it is necessary to return to the griddle…

Grose in 1790 defined a fadge as "a thick cake of an oval shape made of wheaten meal and water and baked upon a griddle." Jamieson's *Scottish Dictionary* of 1802 notes: "a fadge… a large flat loaf or bannock, commonly of barley meal and baked among the ashes." The point of transition seems to have been the first half of the nineteenth century, i.e. when the kitchen range was being introduced. Then John Bell, writing in Newcastle, defined fadges as "thick cakes, baked on girdle or iron plate on the fire." However, on second thoughts, he partly deleted this and amended it to read "fadges – thick cakes, baked in an oven, being too thick to bake on the fire." (Bell, *MS* 12)

The conclusion would seem to be, the flat, round shape of such loaves goes back to the oatcake tradition and the use of a griddle. In the later oven world, if there was surplus dough when the bread tins were filled, what was more sensible than to roll it out flat and bake it on a griddle or in the oven? "On a normal baking day, it would be common practice also to bake a small leavened batch on the bakestone, while the bulk of the dough would be baked in the oven." (Tibbott, p.23) Surplus dough could also be baked while the oven was heating or cooling, or at the oven bottom when it was at full heat. Not being in a tin, rolling out flat would help the dough retain its shape during cooking (on a supporting surface) and help it take advantage of a lower cooking heat (as opposed to the denser shape of a loaf proper).

Fadge and stottie are now baked in commercial ovens and their close texture is achieved by adjusting rising time and temperature – though this is apparently no more than a way of simulating what happened when surplus dough was fitted into the schedule of kitchen range cooking – and that in turn harked back to the traditions of cooking on a flat griddle.

To conclude, a description of the stotty-cake and its art from New Herrington, 1930s:

> When baking bread and if there was sufficient dough left over, or purposely, after the bread tins had been filled, my mother would make stotty-cakes. The size and number being governed by the amount of dough left over.
>
> This was not uncommon as a lot of baking, in those days, was without scales and handfuls were the measure and of course there were big families. It also avoided waste.
>
> Some families preferred and made only stotties. They averaged 8"–9" diameter and ½" thick when rolled out then dusted with flour and placed on the oven bottom. If this followed bread-making then the fire under the oven would be raked out to reduce the heat factor which was only acquired from experience.
>
> Here again experience, as ovens could be variable, told you when to check the rise of the stotty to approximately 1½" thick and whether it was ready to turn over to cook right through. Then cut for eating – it could be with butter, jam, treacle, cheese, meat or dripping.
>
> (C.T.)

Additionally from Seaham, 1930s:

> Stotty-cake was baked in the bottom of the oven, cooked for quickness with only one rising. It was tough!

And from Gateshead:

> Use a stottie cut in half to make a pizza base!

Ned cake

The name probably derives from being 'kneaded' rather than 'needed'. It could be yeast dough or pastry dough, the only point of agreement among informants being that ned cakes were made of leftover dough:

> Ned kyek is pastry as used for pies rolled out about half inch thick, cut in squares about 3 inches, baked then used for sandwiches.
>
> (G.D.)

> I can't give details on what we (in the 1930s) called "ned cakes" other than to say they were dry-textured, tasteless monstrosities that could be eaten only if sliced in half and covered in treacle or condensed milk.
>
> (L.G.)

> (I remember) ned cake as leftovers from pastry cooking and kneaded together to the shape and roughly to size of a cone and cooked from practice/experience. Currants would be added if preferred and they were eaten with butter and jam…
>
> (C.T.)

> "Ned cake" was short-crust pastry – solid round – ate hot with butter as did not keep well.
>
> (M.R.)

> Sometimes lard would be mixed into the dough to make ned cakes.
>
> (Hitchin, 1962, p.20)

Damper Bread

…perhaps deserves a mention. It was an unrisen 'panacke' of flour and water, useful for survival.

> You were wanting to know about damper bread. I know this one from my interest in Ray Mears survival stuff. Damper bread or Australian Damper bread, is unleavened bread best made on a campfire but can be done in an oven using self-raising flour, milk, water, a bit of butter or marge and a pinch of salt. You can add sugar or raisins or summat if you've got them.

> Mix up the ingredients in the usual way for pastry until the mix feels as soft as a baby's arse. Then cook in a covered pan, or if you're inclined on a stick over the fire for about 1/2 hr. I like to use beer in mine instead of water, which gives it a better flavour.
>
> (Chris)

Panackelty

A lovely meal my Mam used to make for us she called 'fanacklty' (sic) – other folk called it 'Panacklty' or 'Panhaggerty'. I've even been told it was called 'Warton Pie' (Wartime pie). Basically it was layers of corned beef, onion and sliced potatoes…

(A.B.)

(Further research indicates that 'Warton' could be 'Woolton' after the Minister for Food in WW2, Lord Woolton, who introduced rationing.) (Other wartime treats were tinned chicken (cooked, whole) or tinned sausages in grease – American donations?)

The secret of panackelty (or however you spell it) seems to be *economy* – of ingredients, effort and time; plus a good deal of versatility and improvisation. An early mention comes from Dalton-le-Dale in the 1910s: "Panacalty – a concoction of bacon, onions and sliced potatoes baked in a shallow dish in the huge oven." (Hitchin, 1962, p.22) It can well be believed it was a popular dish in the lean 1930s and war years that followed.

Its basis is potato – sliced so as to cook easily in a pan. It could be cooked in a frying pan if a little liquid (rather than or as well as oil) was used, and ideally a lid. That would be a good meal for one or two. A larger family pie, with several layers of potato, could be cooked in an oven.

Panackelty was… basically made with alternate layers of thinly sliced potatoes and meat, which could be corned beef, leftovers from joints or bits of bacon. We had it coal-oven baked.

(L.G.)

Here on Teesside, we have panacalty, in my family, corned beef sliced and simmered with parboiled sliced potatoes, peas, gravy and anything else you can hoy into it.

(V.W.)

Panackelty

8 oz raw ham, 1 large onion, potatoes.

Fry ham and onion in frying pan. When cooked, fill frying pan with water and sliced potatoes, leaving in the fat. See that the ham is on top of the potatoes.

Put in salt and pepper to taste. Cover frying pan with lid or large plate.

Cook until potatoes are done then serve hot.

(*Shildon recipe book*, ca. 1935)

Please note, you should not pour cold water onto hot fat! Let the pan cool a bit before adding any other liquid!

Another recipe, this time called:

Pan haggerty

¹/₂ lb onions / 1 lb potatoes / 4 oz grated cheese / 1 tabspn dripping / seasoning.

Cut vegetables into thin slices and pat dry. Heat dripping in pan, add vegetables and cheese in layers, seasoning as you go. Fry gently till cooked and brown under grill.

(N'd Cook Book)

Under the title 'Tatie Stovies', the *Northumberland Cook Book* allows the additions of some finely chopped cold meat; "besides a little dripping, use stock or water almost to cover contents; cook slowly until all liquid absorbed." A dusting of flour would help thicken the stock. The recipe could also use left over cold meat from a Sunday joint – making panackelty a popular meal on a busy Monday.

Lastly, to underline the improvisation:

> Panackelty, surely, was always whatever was left in the house before pay day – uncooked bacon and/or sausage and/or corned beef (which could be bought loose, very cheaply, at Duncan's or Bob Grant's).

> These ingredients, often with the addition of baked beans, were interspersed with layers of sliced potato and onion, finishing with potato on the top, and cooked slowly in the oven for three hours or more.

[www.sunderlandtoday.co.uk]

The gas oven

Though gas cookers were invented in the nineteenth century, there was considerable prejudice against this new mode of cooking (wasn't gas poisonous after all?) and they only became practical and popular in the 1920s. This was helped by the invention of the regulo or thermostat in 1915, and fitted as standard by manufacturers, Radiation, from 1923. Such ovens were more appropriate to the privately built 'suburban' housing of the 1930s than the terrace house or early council property – many models of gas oven had to be rented from the gas company. The detached – some would say isolated – pattern of pit villages in Co. Durham did not encourage the laying on of a gas supply. Especially with so much coal close at hand!

> Gas cookers were slow in appearing because we were a coal orientated area with most people living in rented colliery/council houses. At some collieries some employees had free coal delivered to their homes. I think it is fairly

obvious the [house] owners would not be keen on the expenditure of cooker installation… Most colliery villages would not have had an overall gas supply in use.

(C.T., New Herrington, 1930s)

Gas stoves (as they were known when I was young)… We had one in our newly-built (non-council) house from 1938. It stood on four legs well off the ground so you could get under it to polish the lino. I would swear it didn't have a regulo but I could be wrong. I wasn't encouraged to do any cooking.

(A.K., Newcastle)

Re: Regulo cookers. My parents were married in 1928, I was born in 1931 and we had a cooker with regulo as far back as I can remember… the house was a semi, new when my parents moved in, in 1928 – in Grantham Avenue, West Hartlepool.

(P.E.)

Early gas oven

In Framwelgate, for example, I am told it was not until the 1950s that gas ovens came into common use; many a terrace house was modernised in the 1950s and 1960s, with an extension for an indoor bathroom – and a refitted kitchen! The better (semi-detached) housing of new suburbs round Sunderland and Newcastle no doubt had gas from the start. *But not servants.* A revealing Radiation Cooker advert of 1934 tells a pretty domestic tale:

THE 'REGULO' DOES IT AGAIN!

While the Dinner cooks – the hostess entertains

They know she has no cook – yet she's not a bit worried – she has put the whole meal into her 'New World' Gas Cooker and five minutes is all she needs to dish up. For the 'Regulo' controls the oven-heat and cooks the dinner perfectly.

The shift to gas cookers in the last 50 years or so is a significant move, because of the more-or-less exact control of the oven temperature by the regulo device. Though an experienced cook could do well with an uncontrolled kitchen range, a generation of housewives was to grow up for whom the cookery books, issued in the 1930s onwards by the companies that manufactured the ovens, were to become domestic bibles. Who could resist the switch of a gas tap, to be rewarded by queen cakes (regulo 5, 15–17 minutes) or lamb chops (baked at regulo 6, 25–30 minutes)?

In a busy world, where women were increasingly called on to take employment and servants were increasingly rare, the convenience of eating when you like, the labour saving of gas over coal, the option to have four saucepans boiling at once (all at slightly different heats, too) and the delight of delicacies cooked in minutes must have led to the scrapping of many a faithful old range.

If there was a disadvantage to the gas cooker, it was that the heat came from a specific direction – usually the bottom and back of the oven cavity, but sometimes the sides – unlike the all-round heat of a kitchen range oven with its flues. This meant a gas oven had to be 'warmed' first and also made it advisable to turn food round during the cooking process. However, this small additional art was as nothing to the secret lore of the kitchen range and happily many recipes apply equally to the gas and the coal oven.

A maslin (mixed grain) loaf

1 kg packet of strong wholemeal flour / 3 cups approx. of fine oatmeal / 4 level tisp salt / 2 tisps carraway seeds (optional) / 3 tabspns butter or oil.

Mix and warm dry ingredients (16 or 20 seconds in a microwave should suffice). Add 1 oz live yeast in a little warm water (some types of dried yeast can be mixed in with the dry ingredients rather than needing to be reconstituted). Mix the whole with warm water to a soft coherent dough.

Knead on a floured board, pushing away from you with the heels of the hands, then folding the dough back together and turning it 90 degrees; and repeat the action. Adjust flour/water content as necessary (the dough will often seem sticky at first so wait a little and see.) After 5–10 minutes the dough should achieve an elastic texture, clean and non-sticky – this is the gluten or protein in the flour whose properties are developed by kneading and which serves to rise the dough by capturing the carbon dioxide given off by the action of yeast on carbohydrates.

Place the dough in a bowl. Sprinkle a little spare flour on the surface, cover with a cloth and leave to rise – either in a warm place, or by giving the dough a gentle low-power warm for 10 seconds every 10 minutes in a microwave.

After about half an hour, or when the dough has risen 'to twice its former size', howk it out of the bowl, and 'knock it back', i.e. compress it by knocking the air out of it, then knead it again to regain that elastic consistency (it shouldn't take so long this time). Cut into four parts, pat out to an oblong, then roll up, starting at one of the shorter ends, tucking the roll tightly to exclude any air and form into a neat 'brick' shape. Put into an oiled 1 lb loaf tin (the above should make four loaves about half filling each tin), cover and leave to rise in the warm (about 20–30 minutes – meanwhile heat the oven up). When dough is well risen, e.g. to nearly top of tin, put into the hot oven to bake.

Cook at Mk 8 for 20 minutes, turning after 10 minutes; then knock loaf out of tin and place without tin on bars of oven, upside down, to finish cooking – Mk 7 a further 5–15 minutes. (These precautions are not needed in a fan-assisted oven.) Overall length of cooking depends partly on the heat of the oven, partly on the height of the rungs in the oven, partly on how you position the loaves on the rungs.

To test if cooked – 1. The crust will be a nice brown. 2. The sides and base of the loaf, if pressed, will be resilient, bounce back into shape. 3. If you tap the base of the loaf it should sound 'hollow' (I have never fully understood that test). Then turn the loaf out and place it athwart the empty tin to cool.

If you use fresh yeast, knead well and keep the dough warm, this is surely one of the most fool-proof and satisfying of cooking operations. The inclusion of some fine oatmeal and carraway seeds makes a specially delicious loaf!

Pea pie

The steak and onion were cooked in a stock in an iron pan directly sitting on a LOW coal fire. There were no hooks or bars. (Time? – till it was done!) Then these were transferred into an enamel dish for the steeped peas to be added and then covered with the suet pastry crust. It was then baked in the oven till the pastry was done and brown. I would think given that it was a low fire, that this baking wouldn't be that quick either. I would think that frying in fat on an open fire might have been a wee bit dangerous(!), so I think most cooking involved braising, boiling or baking.

Don't forget that most working-class houses in the colliery districts had a 'kitchen' (living room) fire, with an oven on one side and maybe a boiler for hot water on the other (if it was a good house) – really more of a range than a fire – as the only means of cooking.

(V.R.)

Bacon pastry

1 lb or slightly less, prepared short-crust pastry / sliced cold boiled bacon.

Roll the pastry out into a square; place sliced bacon over one half; fold over, press lightly to exclude air bubbles and crimp round edges; glaze with beaten egg and cook at approx. 30 minutes at Mk 6 till golden brown.

Gooseberry tart

You can use frozen pie crusts from the supermarket to make the job easy. The tart will be better with your own crust, if you can make it, of course. Buy two punnets of gooseberries (12 ounces or 340g) for one 9-inch double crust pie. Wash the gooseberries thoroughly, discarding any yellow berries and other undesirable bits. Do not worry about the brown bits on the berries – you will not notice them in the pie. Mix the berries with about $1/2$ cup of sugar and a tabspn of arrowroot. Arrowroot is a secret ingredient that is better in fruit pies than cornstarch, flour or tapioca for thickening the filling. You can also add a teaspoon of cinnamon if you like. Some recipes have you crush half the gooseberries and cook them a little with the sugar first. Fill the pie shell and put the upper crust on top, pinching the rim to join the crusts. Cut four 2" slits in the top crust.

Put the pie in a 425°F oven (hot) on a baking sheet and cook for about 30–40 minutes, until the top crust is nicely brown and the filling is bubbling. Remove and cool. That's all there is to it! It is good warm or cold, with heavy cream, (English) custard, or just plain.

Plate pie

This is almost any pastry pie, cooked in a heat-resistant plate, e.g. a soup plate or dessert plate – which gives its shape to the pie. The pastry is rolled out, moulded into the plate, filled with apple or what-have-you and a pastry top put on ready for cooking. Using this method, a handy individual size pie can be made, or indeed a range of sizes without having to buy lots of pastry tins. The pie can be served (and eaten) on the plate it's cooked on.

Rice cake

8 oz castor sugar / 6 oz margarine or butter / 6 oz ground rice / 2 oz ground almonds / 2 oz self-raising flour / 3 eggs.

Blend sugar and fat together to a cream (traditionally with a rotating motion of the hand); stir in eggs and gently fold in the dry ingredients. Put into a greased and floured baking tin. Cook Mk 2 for an hour or a little more.

(E.P.)

Shortbread

4 oz flour / 4 oz ground rice / 2 oz sugar / 5 oz margarine.

Mix together flour and ground rice. Cream the margarine and sugar. Work in the flour and ground rice. Knead to a consistent dough. Roll out half an inch think, pinch the edges, prick all over with a fork. Bake in a moderate oven (on a baking tray), but do not brown.

(Shildon recipe book, ca. 1935)

Fruit batter

4 oz self-raising flour / 2 oz butter / 2 oz sugar / pinch of salt / 2 cups of varied fruit / milk to mix.

Rub butter into flour, add sugar and salt. Prepare fruit, e.g. peel and cut cooking apple, chunks of rhubarb, some blackcurrants or blackberries. Mix to a thick batter. Grease an oven dish, spoon the mixture in and cook Mk 6 for 30–40 minutes till risen and light brown.

(Seaham recipe book)

Gingerbread *(a recipe from Kirkbymoorside):*

6 lb flour / 3 lb treacle (melted) / 1 lb lard or butter (melted) / 1 lb brown sugar / 1 oz ground coriander seed / 1 oz ground carraway seed / 1 oz ground cinnamon seed / 1 oz allspice / 1 oz carbonate of soda / $1^{1}/_{2}$ oz ground ginger, pinch salt.

All ingredients had to be warm. Kneaded by hand and cooked in a cool oven (250°) for 3 hours. (Hartley, 1972, p.127). The consistency of the dough was clearly thick, since it would be pressed into moulds to make surface relief patterns on individual slices before cooking.

The range of recipes is endless. Popular in East Durham beside rice cake, were madeira cake, coconut haystacks, fairy cakes, butterfly cakes, caramel (a shortbread with a layer of caramel at its base), cream horns, carraway seed tea-cake, sly cake (a layer of currants between pastry layers), date cake (similar, but with a pastry of oats, butter and suagr – Morpeth) and many more. These are part of the national sorority of the modern oven, not exclusively regional; delicious, though. Rather let us call them North-East preferences: for example, we are said to prefer battenburgs while the South favours swiss rolls. (Allen, p.36)

Modern cooking

The refrigerator

Cooking has not stood still with the perfection of the gas oven (or its twin, the electric oven). In the 1960s, the refrigerator became a novel adjunct to domestic kitchen equipment. This spelt doom for the pantry and the mesh-metal meat safes. Easily milk could be kept cool and fresh even during summer months and encouraged us to eat a range of breakfast cereals with cold milk, like cornflakes and Weetabix (Shredded Wheat I remember as more of a hot milk thing). All thanks to the Milk Marketing Board (1933):

> ...an experiment in an entirely new principle, the marketing of a farm commodity on a national basis by a producer-controlled organization. Operating a monopoloy in the sale of milk, it pooled the receipts and allocated them to producers in price ranges which took account of geography, the calendar and, to some extent, quality... In recent years (1960s) it has, by a clever advertising campaign, boosted the sale of 'liquid' milk to a level far surpassing that in most other countries...
>
> (Whitlock, 1966, p.215)

Curiously, the North East was slow to see the advantage of the fridge and some maintained that tea tasted better with sterilised milk. Nonetheless fridges have helped mould modern food tastes – in keeping salads and yoghurts fresh, for example. Some recipes actually use a fridge for the 'cooking' process...

Trifle

Sponge cake(s) / raspberry jam / 2 bananas / 1 tin apricots / 2 oz cherries / a little almond essence (or sherry or liqueur) / $^1/_2$ pint custard (or 1 pint) / 1 orange / 1 lemon / 1 oz sugar / cream.

Split sponge cakes, spread with jam, cut into small pieces and line bottom of dish. [Slices of a ready-made swiss roll looks good in a glass dish!] Squeeze juice from lemon, orange, (add) apricot (syrup), sugar and essence. Soak sponge cake. Beat apricots and bananas to a pulp. Cover sponge cake with layers of fruit sprinkled with cut cherries. Add custard. Decorate the top (with cream, etc.)

(Shildon recipe book, ca. 1935)

Chocolate truffles

20 fluid ounces cream / 21 oz dark chocolate / 3 oz butter.

Heat all ingredients in a pan to melt, then bring to the boil. Leave to cool, beating frequently to establish texture. When cool, form into rounds and roll in cocoa powder. (Remember to dust your hands in cocoa powder before starting to roll the mix, or the 'cocoa butter' will soon coat them!) Store in fridge to consolidate.

Ice cream

The secret of ice cream is two-fold – the very best natural ingredients and stirring as the mix cools (to eliminate ice crystals and achieve the correct smooth texture). If a typical ice cream takes 2 hours to set, then it is a good idea to give the mix a good beating at least twice during this period. Popular in England since the late nineteenth century and a special favourite in the inter-war years, ice cream has increasingly become a commercial product, traditionally associated with Italian firms. Yet the home enthusiast used to be able to purchase a small bucket-shaped device, with space for ice (bought from the fish-mongers) round the outside and an interior well for the creamy mix. Turning a paddle kept the ice cream mix smooth and crystal-free. By such a machine, I am told, custard made a very passable vanilla ice cream.

Fortunately a basic and delicious ice cream can be made at home without any equipment (other than a freezer compartment). A standard recipe could be: 1 lb blackberries or gooseberries, sweetened and cooked till soft with hardly any water. Mash, sieve and cool. Fold in half-pint double cream, then beat well… and freeze! (But return to the main fridge for 15 minutes before eating, so it is not too hard a texture.) Flavourings can include expresso coffee or melted chocolate…

All fridges included a small freezer compartment ideal for the home production of ice lollies. Foods to fit the freezer compartment were soon available like the famous fish finger (1955). Early in the 1960s this led to some inevitable misunderstandings – you could cook some products from frozen but needed to be prepared for very different cooking times. The same, of course, with those tempting frozen legs and shoulders of lamb from Australia and New Zealand, and the ubiquitous frozen chicken of recent years. *Thaw well* should be our motto.

The big sister of the fridge, the freezer – as a separate unit – became familiar during the 1970s and '80s. It is more of a storage facility than a new food process, but is now a standard way of accessing a handy supply of vegetables, meat and pies – and cutting down on the number of shopping trips you have to make. Fancy sweets of the Black Forest gâteau type that we are unlikely ever to master the cooking of come in frozen form too, and only need thawing out. (Magic eh?)

Other technology

Earlier, and quite at the opposite end of the thermometer, came the deep-frying process. From its inception in the mid-nineteenth century, this has remained essentially a commercial operation – the quantity of oil required and the dangers attaching to extreme hot temperatures make it less ideal for home use. Yet it has made a very special contribution to our repertoire of cooking techniques – the heat means the food is sealed and cooks quickly, retaining full flavour; a coating of breadcrumbs or batter prevents the formation of a tough crust on the food itself and minimises loss of moisture – or in the case of chips, the absence of protection produces a crisp golden outer surface that makes potatoes specially palatable. Unlike other cooking processes, seasoning, e.g. salt needs to be added afterwards. (In the North-East likelier chips 'n' gravy, chips 'n' curry sauce.) (In Holland they favour simple chips with mayonnaise – try it!)

> Gran [from Springwell] would say to me, 'Get away to the fish shop and get me a paper for your grandad.' I thought she meant a newspaper from the newsagent hut next to the fish shop, but it turned out she meant a portion of fish-and-chips wrapped in paper. Our normal order would be 'fish an' a penn'orth o chips' – a whole haddock could be had for tuppence. And there were 'scrapings' as extras.
>
> (F.M., Ashington)

And so to changes in tastes as well as technology and notably the increasing fashion for food from abroad. Chinese restaurants (1960s), Indian (1970s), Italian (1980s) and Thai (1990s) have come in successive waves to tempt our palates. Italian cookery, with its beneficial olive oil, student-friendly spaghetti bolognese, fondness for garlic, attractive sweet courses and universal pizza has surely had the greatest impact on home cooking. No supermarket today is deemed complete without a place for buffalo milk mozzarella cheese.

The terms of foreign cuisine now trip off the tongue, but early in the 1960s the Chinese restaurant was a mystery and something of a dare, as when one opened in Sunderland:

> The colours of the food, in the large oval-shaped bowl the waitress brought me, were beautiful to say the very least. I was enthralled. Seemingly set in a delicate haze, wisps of steam rose from the morsels of nourishment in this "boat of plenty", they carried the aromas, that were making my mouth water. Behind this new experience in the art of culinary excellence, she placed a large plate of plain white rice?
>
> Tucking into the food from the bowl, it was delicious. Pork, chicken, prawns and loads of other stuff, all set in a gorgeous and unbelievably tasty glutinous sauce. I had never had so many different (yet matching) flavours in my mouth at the same time. My taste buds were in heaven.

The waitress came over to the table. Bending down she whispered into my ear, "Excuse me sir, but you usually put the food that is in the bowl, on the rice". Looking at her with eyes that must have spoken of my ignorance I replied, "Woman, do you take me for a pig! I save my rice for afters".

(T.M.)

The appeal of novel food-cultures has been an important factor in encouraging the growth of pre-prepared meals – simple complete meals for one or two people, such as curries, that can be cooked from frozen in a microwave, enabling us all, men and women, to work longer hours at the office.

The microwave oven, which became popular in the 1990s, is (to date) the last word in cooking technology. It can happily defrost frozen foods, even small joints of meat; it can cook vegetables with minimal loss of flavour; it can re-heat food in a trice (though we have learned to avoid re-heating pastry – it only ends up soggy). Best of all, it cooks in minutes a frozen meal so you hardly need to wait to eat when you come in dog-tired from all that overtime at work.

Surprisingly, 'convenience food' is not just a modern idea – at a big rally in Newcastle 1873, "There were scores of stalls for the sale of dear ham sandwiches, cheap toffee, cheap gingerbread, cheap ginger-beer, cheap buns, and fair-priced paste eggs without the dye." (*Newcastle Weekly Chronicle*, 19 April, 1873) However, there is a difference between walking from Durham to Newcastle while snacking on a ham sandwich and lying dead-beat on a settee in front of the telly with your quick-cook meal-tray. Its advantages and disadvantages aside, what the microwave does not seem to have done is prompt much in the way of novel recipes.

Other developments seem more like returns to past practices: small electric 'lean grills' recall the griddle of old; the slow cooker invokes the kitchen range at its best.

One minor but useful invention is the food processor, which not only saves labour (in beating Yorkshire pudding mix or bread dough or cream-based dishes or cake mix), but subtly contributes to our range of foods by making it easy to juice fruit and purée vegetables for soups. They take a bit of cleaning out afterwards – but then, there's always the dishwasher for that!

Nearly done

Is this minimisation of effort getting out of hand? In 1968 it was noted "Tyneside resembled Wales in its wholesale conversion to the handy and expensive tinned and frozen foods." (Allen, p.177) Urbanisation has led to the loss of many wholesome traditional foods and the mass marketing of sliced bread and neat sausages in the mid-twentieth century further degraded our palates. Today we are faced with stark choices: healthy organic food with exercise as part of a sensible diet or more fast food and its consequences. Food has become very much part of our concern for health and it looks as if our future tastes may well be shaped by doctors and laboratory researchers rather than chefs.

An eminent professor I once knew was invited to dinner with Tony Benn. Over a glass of sherry before the meal, wor Tony remarked that he supposed with all this progress, they would hardly need to eat in some future age, just take a pill or two, and receive thus all the nutriment a human could need. My professor friend disagreed profoundly: cooking and eating to him was a special and rewarding social experience.

He's right of course. Nothing can beat fresh ingredients suitably cooked and brought 'piping hot' (as the phrase is) to the table. Simpler the better. It makes the moderate time taken in preparation worthwhile – get everyone to join in! – it won't spoil the broth – and the final gains in flavour and nutrition are just as important as the fun of sitting down with family or friends to enjoy a meal in good company. The Anglo-Saxon warrior band in thatched hut, the Medieval knight and his lady in hall, the Tudor family at their new wide-chimney hearth, the Methodists with their bring-and-share 'faith suppers', the hard-working pitman's wife at her kitchen range – all insist it is so and you wouldn't want to argue with them, would you?

Sources/References

Atkinson, J. A. *et al.* (1993) *Darlington Wills 1600–1625*, Surtees Society vol. 201.

Allen Elliston, D. (1968) *British Tastes: an enquiry into the likes and dislikes of the regional consumer*. London.

Allingham, H. & D. (1909) Stewart *The Cottage Homes of England*. London.

Armstrong, K. & White, V. (eds) (1977) *Sweets for my sweet: the story of Welch's sweets, the North Tyneside family firm*. Whitley Bay.

Bailey, J. (1810) *General View of the Agriculture of Co. Durham*.

Baldock, D. (1995) *A taste of Northumbria: Northumberland, Durham and Geordie-land. A selection of traditional local recipes*. Sevenoaks.

Baxter, E. (1974) *Ena Baxter's Scottish Cookbook*. Edinburgh.

The British Minstrel (Durham, 1839).

Brockett, W. (1846) *North Country Words*. Newcastle.

Brown, R. (2003) 'Illuminating the Twentieth Century: a short history of gas lighting' PhD, Northumbria University.

Carron Kitchen Ranges (1908) *Catalogue*. Stirlingshire.

Catcheside-Warrington, C. E. (1917) (ed.) *Tyneside Stories and recitations*. Newcastle.

A collection of traditional recipes from County Durham (Story of Seaham Group, 1996).

Crocker, J. (1983) *Accent on the North East: Dialect jottings*. Darlington.

Curtis, R. I. (2001) *Ancient Food Technology*. Leiden.

Life of St Cuthbert in English Verse ca. AD 1450 (Surtees Society vol.98, 1891).

Denham M. A. (1974) *Tracts* (repr. Newcastle).

Egglestone, W. (1870) 'Betty Podkins at the Crook Exhibition' *Durham Chronicle* 25 March.

Eveleigh, D. (1986) *Old Cooking Utensils*. Aylesbury.

Eveleigh, D. (1983) *Firegrates and Kitchen Ranges*. Aylesbury.

The Everyday Book (1827) London.

Field, R. (1984) (sic) *Irons in the Fire: a history of cooking equipment*. Marlborough.

Hagan, A. (1992) *A handbook of Anglo-Saxon Food*. Thetford.

Hartley, M. & Ingleby, J. (1972) *Life in the Moorlands of North-East Yorkshire*. London.

Heath, V. (1995) *Canny Geordie Cook Book*. Newcastle.

Hitchin, G. (1962) *Pit-Yacker*. London.

Holland, N. (1956) *Sea Harvest* (Unilever).

Howey, P. (1971) *The Geordie Cook Book*. Newcastle.

HRCM – Historical Review of Coal Mining (1924) London: Mining Assoc. of GB.

Hudson, M. (1994) *Coming Back Brockens*. London.

The Kitchen Catalogue (Castle Museum, York, 1979).

Latimer, J. (1857) *Local Records*. Newcastle.

MacDonald, G. (1882) *Castle Warlock*. London.

Marshall, T. (1829) *A collection of original local songs*. Newcastle.

Meadows, C. A. (1978) *The Victorian Ironmonger*. Aylesbury.

Meadows, C. A. (1984) *The Victorian Ironmonger* (2nd edn). Aylesbury.

Moffatt Brothers (Gateshead) *Ranges, etc.* (und.).

Moorman, F. W. (ed.) (1916) *Yorkshire Dialect Poems*. London.

'A Northumbrian Bake-stick' *Monthly Chronicle*, Nov. 1889, p.2. Newcastle.

Northumbrian Words and Ways (vol.3) Compiled by Jean Crocker (1990).

Northumberland Cook Book (Northumberland Federation of Women's Institutes, ca. 1950).

Parker, J. (1896) *Tyne Folk*. London.

Pearce, D. *Spot the Fireplace* (National Trust, und.).

Beatrix Potter (1907) *The Tale of Tom Kitten*. London.

Beatrix Potter (1912) *The Tale of Mr Tod*. London.

Raine, J. (1837) *Deeds of Finchale Priory*, Surtees Society vol.6.

'Regional Recipes from the North East', *Mrs Beaton* (magazine) 1990, pp.60–63.

Robson, W. J. (1890) *The Adventures of Jackie Robison*. Newcastle.

Sharp, C. (1834) *The Bishoprick Garland, or a collection of legends, songs, ballads, etc., belonging to the County of Durham*. Sunderland.

Seymour Lindsay, J. (1927) *Iron & Brass Implements of the English House*. London.

Shields Song Book (1826) South Shields.

Shildon Church Methodist Circuit. *Your favourite recipe book* (ca. 1935).

Slack, M. (1981) *Northumbrian Fare*. Newcastle.

Smylie, M. (2004) *Herring: A history of the silver darlings*. Stroud.

Stainthorpe, F. (ca.2001) *Home and Away*. Shotton.

The Story of Seaham Group (1996) *A collection of traditional recipes from County Durham*. Seaham.

Stukeley, W. (1776) *Itinerarium curiosum*. London.

Tannahill, R. (1988) *Food in History* (Penguin).

Tibbott Minwell, S. (1982) *Cooking on the Open Hearth* (National Museum of Wales).

Webster, T. (1861) *An Encyclopaedia of Domestic Cookery*. London.

White, F. (1932, 1962) *Good thing to eat in England*. London.

Whitelock, Ralph (1966) *A Short History of Farming in Britain*. London: Country Book Club.

Wright, L. (1964) *Home fires burning: a history of domestic heating and cooking*. London.

Yorkshire dialogue between an awd wife, a lass, and a butcher (1673) repr. in Moorman (1916).

Result of food survey (North East, 2006)

A general conclusion might be (though this question was not directly asked) that the amount of time spent on food at home and the status of the kitchen has decreased over the last 50 years. Asked what tradtional fare they cook for themselves, only porridge and scones, both relatively simple dishes, scored highly; then (in decreasing order) rice pudding, jams, fruit loaf, pastry, plate pie, bread and chips. For younger respondents only porridge, scones and chips scored.

Only one cooked meal a day was reported, as against the perception of a high calory intake in earlier times. Adults ate out on average once a week; and took advantage of Chinese, Indian and Italian restaurants, and at home, of pre-frozen meals.

In other ways too, traditional habits have moved on. Few of the arts of open fire cooking or the griddle are kept up. No one really makes or uses oatcakes – the oven equivalent, the scone, is preferred. Sweets and puddings have yielded to yoghurts. Two very traditional foods scored highly – bacon among the meats and fish in general, where cod scored highest, then haddock, then salmon. Butter held its own against the various margarines and spreads. Other traditional dishes, however, scored quite low, even with older respondents: leak pudding, black pudding and panackelty had relatively few supporters.

Of breads, wholemeal was reported the great favourite (yet shops seem to stock equal brown and white, and a miner's bait was typically white bread sandwiches; nationally the consumption of white bread is four times that of brown/wholemeal). Stotties seem seldom to be home-made, but can be purchased at commercial bakers, and were admired for their special texture and flavour. Toast was a popular breakfast item; the favourite topping was cheese, with a small vote for marmite or marmalade. Otherwise cereals were a main breakfast favourite, and porridge (esp. in winter), and on a lesser rank, eggs and bacon. Only one respondent owned up to eggs, bacon, beans, sausage, black pudding and fried bread.

Sandwiches featured as a popular lunch (midday meal), cheese or ham the likely fillings, but there was some inventiveness here, e.g. banana and date, ham and pease pudding as fillings. Alternative lunches were soup or a little salad. A few named a midday meal as the main meal of the day – an agricutural tradition?

The main meal was commonly dubbed 'dinner' and eaten about 6 p.m., i.e. after work. The menu was very varied, as one might expect with the wide range of foodstuffs available today. Declared favourites were curries, stews (with dumplings), gammon and chips, sausage and mash, steak and kidney pie, and (especially eaten out) fish and chips. High purchase rates of bacon, canned peas, canned tomatoes, corned beef, leeks, turnips, baked beans, sausages, eggs, salad veg, and frozen veg, are also pointers. The roast joint remains the ideal, with beef a clear favourite, and lamb second. (Against a national preference for poultry.) The conventional twentieth century turkey, convenient for large numbers of diners, was commonest as Christmas dinner.

For puddings, fruit crumble was top, followed by rice pudding and treacle sponge.

In particular categories, what may well be regional favourites emerged. Among large cakes, fruit cake (fruit loaf) emerged a clear favourite (I put rice cake). For smaller cakes, the butterfly cake scored highest (I put snowball). In biscuits, ginger nuts were a clear favourite, then choclate biscuits, then shortbread.

Among fesh fruits, oranges, apples and bananas prevailed. For tinned fruit, sliced peaches came top, then pineapple, then pear. For jams, there was a wide range, but raspberry, blackcurrant and strawberry were favourites.

For root vegetables there was a clear vote for the carrot; joint second were the turnip and the parsnip. Of green veg, cabbage scored highest: in second rank were broccoli, sprouts and peas. Leeks, turnips and pease pudding featured high on the lists of what to purchase.

For sauce on fried food, tomato ketchup came out top, over brown sauce, contrary to the popular concept of the North.

Amongst confections, chocolate and plain chocolate were the favourite, with a smaller vote for toffee and licorice ('spenish'). The strange question – what is your favourite flavour? – turned up the strange answer – (pepper)mint. Most shopped at a supermarket at least once a week. As to whether they favoured low-sugar, low-fat, low-salt foods, most replied yes, but very few would consult their doctor about diet.

Drinks ended in a clear peference for tea: almost twice as many votes as coffee. Tea-bags predominated over loose tea; instant coffee over ground coffee; and bottled water has started making inroads.

Finally, to compare with D. Elliston Allen's 1968 survey – there is some confirmation of the preferences of that time, e.g. biscuits, root veg, leeks, butter beans, fish-cakes, malt bread, canned tomatoes, bacon, plus as noted before "an astounding capacity (and presumably liking) for canned peas, a quite exceptional demand for corned beef and by far the heaviest consumption in the country of brown bread."

Present-day responses from the young showed a measure of agreement with the adult preferences. (Nationally, older people eat more and spend more on food per capita than those under forty-five, e.g. on fresh meat, butter, cakes, confectionary, tea – but less on cereals and soft drinks.) Notable in younger reponses were bananas as favourite fruit; cod and tuna among the fish; carrot and broccoli as veg; an equal use of tea (bags), coffee (instant) and coke (diet); only porridge and chips were commonly cooked at home, among traditional dishes, plus spaghetti bolognese and other pasta dishes; favourite meals out were Indian, Chinese, Italian and Mexican. The most novel sandwich suggestion was humous with carrot and apple. Few mentioned the pizza but occular evidence suggests they are common on the frozen food shelf and easiest of the phone-and-order ready-to-eat items.

Note: including data from D. Elliston Allen (1968) *British Tastes: an enquiry into the likes and dislikes of the regional consumer* (London: Hutchinson, pp.172–4) and DEFRA website National Food Survey 2000, 2003–4.

'Mr Harry Dunn, butcher' by Jimmy Forsythe (1958).

Tyne & Wear Archive Service. P.5/131.

Part three – a glossary in subject sections

An assumption might be, that as Vikings tended to settle the higher land in the west of the region, that words related to pastoral farming might come largely from Old Norse, those of arable farming from Old English. There is limited confirmation of this: the vocabulary of sheep and pig has many words from Old Norse; for cattle and pasturage there is more of an OE element. The ON words for oats and barley are prominent in the region. With the increasing use of tractors in agriculture from the 1930s on, a whole swathe of words relating to manual and horse-driven labour would be expected to fall into neglect. What is remembered of farming terms by correspondents today is marked here (B) for Barnard Castle, (H) for Houghton-le-Spring, (T) for Teesdale.

Dialect terms for animals and crops are not well known in modern urban areas though sometimes reflected in children's words, e.g. cushie, guissie-pig and colley.

There is a good proportion of ON words in the vocabulary of the fire and fireplace, and of household utilities; but the general picture is of an admixture of ON and OE terms, for the languages had long been combined.

Although technological change from early times to eithteenth century were considerable (open wood fire to side-wall coal fireplace) there was a basic continuity of vocabulary. What changed this seems to have been the purpose-built mining village and the kitchen range, bringing a change in technology, terminology and attitude. Some traditional terms are reapplied, e.g. claggum for toffee, but many new ones need to be found, e.g. panackelty (a savoury dish), tidy betty (fender), etc. The switch away from the traditional seems to have begun earlier in the kitchen than in the mining world where major technological changes came slowly in the twentieth century.

Abbreviations in glossary

AN – Anglo-Norman	cf. compare (i.e. not directly derived from)
Du. – Dutch	imit. Imitative (of a natural sound)
Fr – French	Gael. – Gaelic i.e. Scottish/Irish
G'head – Gateshead	Ice – Icelandic
N'd – Northumberland	Newc – Newcastle
Norw. – Norwegian	OE – Old English (Anglo-Saxon)
OFr – Old French	ON – Old Norse (Viking)
S'd – Sunderland	

1. The small holding

2. The kitchen

3. Food

1. *The small holding*

allotment – common form of renting a plot of land for miners and others to cultivate. Present in the nineteenth century, but especially available from local councils 1922 on. (B)(H).

arles – fees paid by masters and mistresses to bind hired servants to their oral contracts, Robson N'd C19/2.

croft – a small inclosure attached to a dwelling house, and used for pasture, tilage, or other purpose. Brockett/Nth C19/1. [OE croft 'field']. (B)(H).

garth – a small enclosure adjoining to a house, Brockett/Nth C19/1; a small yard of field enclosed with a hedge or wall and lying close to a house, Jarrow, *Raine MS*; paddock, Dinsdale/Tees 1849; a small grass-field, enclosed, near a dwelling, Palgrave/Hetton 1896; **applegarth, tettygrath, stag-garth** – stackyard, Hull/wNewc 1880s; **kail-garth** – a kitchen-garden, a cabbage garth, though often adorned with a profusion of flowers, Brockett/Nth C19/1. [ON garthr 'yard'] (B)(H).

hind – an upper farm servant, who generally resides in the farm and has more or less authority over the farm and the ordinary labourers who work upon it: 'the hynde or steward to Mr Butler', Tynemouth, 1680/81 *Raine MS*; a yearly farm servant, Luckley/Alnwick; agricutural labourer, Blenkin/Shildon C20/2. [ME hine 'farm labourer' plus Sco/Nth 'skilled farm worker'] (B)(H)(T).

Poultry

banty – bantam hen. [Bantam in Java] (B)(H)(T).

bauk – hen-bawks – the bawks or cross poles or sticks in a hen-house [Northern], Kennet MS 1695; a hen balk is a perch for hens to sit on, *Bell MS* C19/1. [ON bálkr 'beam'].

bubbly Jock – a turkey cock, *Bell MS* C19/1, Luckley/Alnwick 1870s [?rhyming slang] (B).

cawel – a hen-coop, Heslop/Tyne 1880s. [OE cawl 'basket'].

chucky – a chicken, a hen, Atkinson/Cleveland 1863, Dinsdale/Tees 1849; a young fowl. Palgrave/Hetton 1896; **chucky-egg** Oxnard/Hetton 1990s. [imitative] (B)(T).

chum – used by some stock breeders to indicate that an egg was infertile. Norman Wilson, Newburn.

cletchin' – brood of chickens, Palgrave/Hetton 1896. [ON klekja 'to hatch'] (T).

clocking-hen – a hen desirous of sitting to hatch chickens, Brockett/Nth C19/1; clock – to sit, of hens. 'She's not gan to clock yet', 'Yon hen's clockin', Palgrave/Hetton 1896. [OE cloccian 'to cluck'] (B)(H)(T).

cree – shed for pigeons, Blenkin/Shildon C20/2. [? from creel] (B)(H)(T).

crowdy – bran mash, e.g. for rabbits or hens, Blenkin/Shildon C20/2; crowdy only hen food, South Moor (Stanley) 2003, Belmont 2006 [cf. Ice groutr 'porridge'] (B)(H)(T).

ducket – (pigeon) shed, Dobson 7. [dove-cot] (H).

geslings – goslings, *Bell MS* C19/1. [OE, ON] (B)(T).

gyus – a goose, *Bell MS* C19/1. [OE gós] (B).

hobby – goose (child's term), Dinsdale/Tees 1849. [also used of a horse and a falcon]; **ob-ee ob-ee** – call or summons for the geese, Atkinson/Cleveland 1863.

ken-specked – markt or branded with spots or speckles [Northern], Kennet MS 1695; **kenspecked, kenspeckled** – conspicuous; specked, so as to be easily kenned, Brockett/Nth C19/1. (B)(T).

mawzy – a speckled hen, Heslop/Tyne 1880s. [from maze i.e. confused pattern].

penker – small egg, the first egg(s) of a pullet, Blenkin/Shildon C20/2. [cf. penker 'large marble' ?from spanker] (B)(H).

plote – to pluck (a fowl), Dinsdale/Tees 1849; ploat – [to] pluck feathers off hen, etc., Blenkin/Shildon C20/2. [Flem/Du ploten] (B)(H)(T).

poomers – large eggs, N'd ca.1950 per FW.

quex – a brood goose, *Bell MS* C19/1.

steg – a gander, Grose 1787, Atkinson/Cleveland 1863, Dinsdale/Tees 1849; a steige, a gowse, withe her broddele, Connescliffe 1553 via D'm, *Raine MS*.; 'I am neyther goos-steler nor steg steiler' Sedgefield ca.1570 via D'm, *Raine MS*; 'as cross as onny steg' ca.1814 Harker/Tyne. [ON steggi] (B)(T).

storkened / sturkent / starkent – stengthened, set up: 'weel storkened' (of raising chicks), Heslop/Tyne 1880s. [OE stearc 'strong'] (T).

strinkle – to scatter grain down to fowls: 'strinkle a handful of corn to them' *Bell MS* C19/1. [source unknown; cf. sprinkle] (T).

'thraain – an' reein' (a fowl's neck) Heslop/Tyne 1880s. [OE thráwan 'to twist', OE writhian 'to turn'].

Sheep

drought'n ewes – sorting the old ewes out, them wi broken mooths 'n bad bags, D.G., Hexhamshire.

gimmer – a female sheep from the first to the second shearing, Brockett/Nth C19/1. [ON gymbr] (B)(H)(T).

hog – a sheep in its state from a lamb to its first shearing; after which it is a **dinmont** if a wedder and a **gimmer** if a ewe, Brockett/Nth C19/1. [source unknown] (B)(H)(T).

kebbed ewe – ewe that has aborted her lamb; **keb hoose** – little shed used for setting lambs on, D.G., Hexhamshire.

kessen – overturned or unable to get up, Upper Teesdale 2001; cassen – of a sheep… cast upon its back and unable to rise, Heslop/Tyne 1880s; cassen, kessen – thrown down, as applied to an animal… that has fallen… and is unable to rise again, Atkinson/Cleveland 1863. [ON kasta 'to cast'] (B)(T).

poke – swelling under the jaw caused by the liver fluke, D.G., Hexhamshire.

rud / ruddle – red paint or red ochre used for marking sheep, Heslop/Tyne 1880s. [ruddy] (B)(H)(T).

sauwy sauwy – sheep call, D.G., Hexhamshire.

stell – round stone enclosure for sheep, D.G., Hexhamshire.

tup – a ram Atkinson/Cleveland 1863; a 'tupe' or 'teup' is a ram, Palgrave/Hetton 1896. [cf. Norw/Sw tupp 'cock-hen'] (B)(H)(T).

wear – to keep off: 'wear the sheep oot o' the turnips' Luckley/Alnwick 1870s. [OE warian].

whinnets – balls of muck on a sheep's backside, D.G., Hexhamshire.

Pigs

bran – a boar, a male pig, Heslop/Tyne 1880s; brawn – a boar killed and prepared for the table by salt and other condiments; also a common Northern name for the live animal: 'The Brawn of Brancepeth' Brockett Nth C19/1. [?Fr bran].

cradle – a pig's ladder, Palgrave/Hetton 1896. [cradle in sense of supporting structure].

crit – the smallest of a litter, etc. Heslop/Tyne 1880s. [critter] (H).

gilt – young female pig, Upper Teesdale 2001. [ON gyltr] (B)(H).

giss – pig, Barnard Castle 2001; **gissy** – pet name for a pig, **gissy pig**, Blenkin/Shildon C20/2; **grice, grise** – a pig [Yorks], *Kennet MS*, 1695; **giss-giss** – used when calling for a free pig, Blenkin/Shildon C20/1. [ON gríss 'pig'] (B)(H)(T).

grunge – to grunt, Palgrave/Hetton 1896. [var. of grunt].

hog – a male of the pig kind, Atkinson/Cleveland 1863. [source unknown] (B)(H).

leg cleek – stick used for catching, especially hogs, D.G., Hexhamshire.

pig bin – a bin for the collection of any food waste to be fed to pigs. Norman Wilson, Newburn

recklin – the runt of a pig litter, VW re rural Teesside C20/2. [?ON recklingr 'an exile'] (B).

wattles – teat-like excrescences which hang from the cheeks of some swine, Bailey/Co. D'm 1810. [source unknown] (H)(T).

Wild food animals

a hang – snare for rabbits, D.G., Hexhamshire.

bee-bike – a wild bee's nest, Atkinson/Cleveland 1863; byke – a bee's nest, Brockett/Nth C19/1. [bee-wick i.e. dwelling].

bee skep – a beehive made of straw, Heslop/Tyne 1880s; this is the old-fashioned straw bee-hive …formed of a straw rope about 3/4 inch in diameter which is put into coils that are wrapped and sewn together…" Robson N'd C19/2. [ON skeppa 'basket'] (B)

bumler – a bumble or humble bee, *Bell MS* C19/1. (B)(H)(T).

bunny – a rabbit, *Bell MS* C19/1. (B)(H).

cushat – wild pigeon, Blenkin/Shildon C20/2; used for a wood pigeon when we were bird nesting in Hawthorn Dene; also less interestingly as '**woodies**', Sanderson/Easington 1950s; **cushat** or **cowshut** – the ring dove or wood pigeon, Brockett/Nth C19/1. [OE cusceote] (B)(H)(T).

grey-hen – the black grouse, Heslop/Tyne 1880s. (B).

moorhen – the red grouse, 'The bonny moorhen' (1818 song) (B)(H).

pautrick – partridge, Dinsdale/Tees 1849.

skemmie – 'would be a poor bird, a bird below standard' South Moor (Stanley) 2003. [source unknown] (B).

skep – a hive for bees, also measure for corn etc… made of ropes of straw fastened together with the tough bark of hazels, etc. *Bell MS* C19/1. [ON skeppa 'basket'] (B).

snickle, sniggle – a snare or wire for the capture of hares or rabbits, Atkinson/Cleveland 1863. [related to snag].

Cattle

beal – to roar, to bellow, Brockett/Nth C19/1. [OE bellan, ON belja] (B)(T).

beece – store-cattle (bullocks). Orange/Bebside.

beeld – the shelter for cattle. Beelds for sheep, etc. are common on the high moors in Northumberland, Heslop/Tyne 1880s; **beild** – sheltered as 'it has good beild' *Bell MS* C19/1. [esp. Scots,, C15 on].

beeldy – warm, sheltered from wind: 'a beeldy place' Luckley/Alnwick 1870s.

bense – a cow's stall, Brockett/Nth C19/1. [source unknown, but cf. Gm Banse 'barn'].

blare – to cry aloud, as 'the cow blares,' etc. *Bell MS* C19/1; **blaring** – crying peevishly: 'You'r blaring like a calf' Luckley/Alnwick 1870s. [Du blaren, Fr pleurer] (B)(T).

bracken, brecken – the braken fern *Pteris aquilina*, L... It is regularly harvested for the bedding of cattle, Heslop/Tyne 1880s. [assumed ON brakni] (B)(H)(T).

buse – ox-boose – ox/cow stall for winter nights, Ray/North 1673; cowstand, pig cree, pig stye *Bell MS* C19/1; **boose** – now the upper part of the stall where the fodder lies [Brockett] Heslop/Tyne 1880s. [OE bósih in Lindisfarne Gloss] (T).

byre, byer – cowhouse, Dinsdale/Tees 1849, Heslop/Tyne 1880s, etc. [OE byre] (B)(H).

cow-up – cry to bring cows in from field for milking, Blenkin/Shildon C20/2. (H).

crummy – a favorite name for a cow with crooked horns, Brockett/Nth C19/1. [OE crump 'crooked'].

cushie – cow (child's term) Dinsdale/Tees 1849; **cushy cow** – [childish name for a cow] Luckley/Alnwick 1870s. [cf. ON kús kús! milkmaid's call] (B)(H)(T).

duffit – a sod; **duffit-theaked** – thatched with sods, Heslop/Tyne 1880s. [divot].

edish – fog, aftermath: 'in edyshe tyme' Knaresborough, C16/mid *Raine MS*. [OE edisc 'pasture'].

fog, fogg – the grass grown in autumn after the hay is mown, the second crop, or aftermath, Brockett/Nth C19/1; the clover or second crop that follows a hay crop, Heslop/Tyne 1880s. [source unknown] (B)(H)(T).

fother – feedstuff, Noah Play C15. [OE fóther 'cartload', or cf. fodder] (B)(H)(T).

friscnett – 'frisknett, that is to saye a stott and a guye' Thirlewall, 1582/83 *Raine MS*. [source unknown].

garsil – hedging wood, Bailey/Co. D'm 1810. [ON gertha 'fence'].

gate or gait – a right of pasturage for cattle through the summer, Brockett/Nth C19. [ON gata 'road, way'] (B).

gers – grass [Northern] *Kennet MS* 1695; **girse** – grass Dinsdale/Tees 1849. [OE gærs].

graip – a three-pronged dung fork, Luckley/Alnwick 1870s. [ON græip] (H)(T) (B: gripe).

hain – to save: 'Thor grass fields are a' hained for the cows to gan in' Luckley/Alnwick 1870s. [ON hegna 'to save, protect'].

hawf hawf – cow shout, D.G., Hexhamshire.

hawkie – a white-faced cow, also a general pet-name for the cow, Heslop/Tyne 1880s. [source unknown].

hay heck – along back wall of hemmel, D.G., Hexhamshire.

hemmel – a shed for cattle, &c, Bailey/Co. D'm 1810; 'And in Dunelm, any place covered over head and open on both sides is call'd a hemle or hemble' *Kennet MS* 1695; **helm** or **hemmell** – a barn or shed made of wood to hold hay or corn: 'a long helme with propes, overthwartes, sidetrees & skelbourses, with a heck' Rain, 1626 via York; shelter with sod walls, Hartley. **hemmel** – outhouse of shed for cattle, frequently open in the front, to which they retreat in bad weather as well as to be hand fed, Robson N'd C19/2. [ON heimile 'homestead', cf. OE helm 'helmet, protection'] (B)(H)(T)

hipe – to rip or gore with the horns of cattle, Bailey/Co. D'm 1810. [source unknown] (B)(T).

hopple – to tie the legs together, Bailey/Co. D'm 1810. [source unknown; hobble is var. of hopple] (B)(H)(T).

ing – pasture or meadow lands, low and moist, Atkinson/Cleveland 1863; ings – low wet grounds, Bailey/Co. D'm 1810. [ON eng 'grassland'].

kye – cattle, cows: 'milk t'kye' Egglestone/Weardale C19/2; ky, kye or kie – the plural of cow Brockett/Nth C19/1. [OE cý (pl.)] (T).

leazes – common pasture belonging to the freemen of Newcastle, Brockett/Nth C19/1; gently sloping fields, Dinsdale/Tees 1849. [OE læs(we) 'pasture, commonland'] (B).

lib – to castrate, Bailey/Co. D'm 1810. [OE libban, 'to doctor'].

loan – a place for milking cows: 'the cow loan' Luckley/Alnwick 1870s. [var. of lane].

mistall – a byre or cowhouse: 'the mistalls & other outhouseing' Cambersworth, 1671 via York, *Raine MS*. [source unknown].

nowt – cows and oxen, Grose 1787; Darlington Nowt Fair, Dinsdale/Tees 1849; **nolt** or **nout** – neat cattle, Bailey/Co. D'm 1810. [ON naut].

ousen – oxen, Ray/North 1673. [var. of oxen].

quey, quy – generally pronounced whye – a heifer or young cow until it has had a calf. Finchale Glossary, 1538 via Brockett/Nth C19/1; quey – a heifer, Upper Teesdale 2001. [ON kvíga].

rice – hedging wood, Bailey/Co. D'm 1810; **rice/rise** – twigs, as tree tops or birchwood, used for fencing, etc.: 'a stake and rice fence' Heslop/Tyne 1880s. [OE hrís].

roarashon – "boss's wife would always say, what a roarashon, when the calves were spained, the amount of noise the cows made," D.G., Hexhamshire [<oration]

rowt, rawt – to lowe like ox or cow, Grose 1787; **rowting** – bellowing of ox, Bailey/Co. D'm 1810. [ON rauta] (B)(T).

shield, shiel, shieling – originally a temporary hut of cabin for those who had the care of sheep on the moors, Brockett/Nth C19/1. [ME schéle, cf. ON skíol 'a shelter'].

shippen – a cow-house, Ray/North 1673; a cow-house… byre is the more usual term, Heslop/Tyne 1880s. [OE scypen] (B).

sicaaf – a call to cattle. Orange/Bebside.

skaling – to dress on clean grass land in the Spring intended to be laid away for meadows, *Bell MS* C19/1. [source unknown].

skep – cattle-feeder, Teesdale 2001. [ON skeppa 'basket'] (B).

spaned – weaned, Bailey/Co. D'm 1810; sp'yan – to wean, to take off mother's milk, Dinsdale/Tees 1849. [OFr espanir] (B).

steer – a three-year-old ox, Bailey/Co. D'm 1810. [OE stéor] (B)(H).

a stint – in stocking grass land is equal to an ox or cow's grass, Bailey/Co. D'm 1810. (B).

stirk – a yearling ox or heifer, Bailey/Co. D'm 1810; a **sturk, styrk** – a young bullock or heifer [Northern] *Kennet MS* 1695. [OE stirc 'calf'] (B)(H).

stot – a castrated ox of any age up to the second year and unbroken to the yoke, Heslop/Tyne 1880s; **stottes** – male cattle from one to four years old (1363–4) Raine/Finchale. [OE stot, ON stútr].

whye or quey – a heifer, Bailey/Co. D'm 1810; **wye-calf** – a heifer, Atkinson/Cleveland 1863. [ON kviga].

wise – to leave or let go: 'open the gate, an' wise oot the kye' Luckley/Alnwick 1870s. [OE wísian 'to guide'].

Arable

bauks or **balks** – the grass ridges dividing ploughed lands, properly those in common fields, Brockett/Nth C19/1. [OE balca 'ridge'].

berrier – a thresher, Bailey/Co. D'm 1810.

berry – to thrash out corn: 'Wull is berrying in the barn' Brockett/Nth C19/1; berry (pronounced barry) – to thresh by flail, Heslop/Tyne 1880s. [ON berja 'to hit, thresh'].

clooty-hat – a bonnet for field work, Heslop/Tyne 1880s. [cloot – patch of cloth] (B).

dess – when cutting louse hay in a stackwith a hay spade, when you got to the stack bottom you would start a new dess, D.G., Hexhamshire.

flaa craw – a stick stuck in the middle of a field or garden and dressed with old cloaths to frighten birds, *Bell MS* C19/1. (T).

fur – a furrow: 'rig-and-fur' Brockett/Nth C19/1. [OE furh, ON for] (B)(H)(T).

gaiting – a sheaf of corn set up on end to dry, Bailey/Co. D'm 1810. [?gait = single sheaf].

hack – a strong two-toothed pick-axe or hoe, much used in agriculture, Brockett/Nth C19/1. [ME – fom verb?] (T).

kemp – to strive against each other in reaping corn – rarely for any other superiority, Brockett/Nth C19/1; kempers – the competitors, Brockett/Nth C19/1; campin, kempin – the race in which one [reaper] strove to finish his rig first [ended 1870s] Heslop/Tyne 1880s. [OE campian 'to compete', ON keppa].

kile of hay – a haycock, a small heap, *Bell MS* C19/1. (H).

lee, lay – ploughed land; **lee rigg** – ridge, *Bell MS* C19/1. [OE léa] (H)(B: ley).

look – to pick out weeds from among the growing corn, Atkinson/Cleveland 1863; lowk – to weed corn Ray/North 1673. [OE lúcan] (H).

mow – to stack or pile up (corn in a barn) Dinsdale/Tees 1849. [from noun: OE múwa, ON múge 'a stack'] (B)(T).

mow, as in cow – when stacking hay in a hay shed you would start a new mow when one eye was full, D.G., Hexhamshire.

opin oot – cut around the corn field with scythes before the binder went in, D.G., Hexhamshire.

pike – a large haycock, often six feet high. The small haycocks only are called 'cocks.' Palgrave/Hetton 1896. [cf. Norw. pík 'mountain peak'] (B)(H)(T).

quickens or quicken grass – a general name for all creeping or stoloniferous grasses or plants, which give the farmer so much trouble to eradicate, Bailey/Co. D'm 1810. [OE cwic 'alive'] (B: or whicken).

rig – a ridge, an eminence; **rig-and-fur, rig-and-rein** – ridge and furrow, Brockett/Nth C19/1. [ON hryggr, OE hrycg] (B)(H)(T).

samcast – two ridges ploughed together, Bailey/Co. D'm 1810. [sam/same 'together'].

shear – to reap or cut corn with the sickle. [But] a sheep-shearing is a clipping, Brockett/Nth C19/1; **sheer** – to reap or cut, Bailey/Co. D'm 1810. [OE scieran, ON skera 'to cut'] (H)(T).

threave – 24 sheaves of corn, &c. Bailey/Co. D'm 1810. [cf. Ice. threfi].

Grains

ang or **awn** – the beard growing out of barley, rye, or wheat, Brockett/Nth C19/1. [ON agnar (pl.)] (H)(B: awn); "to speak wi' bunch o' bear-awms in his hause" (barley beards in the throat) Denham Tracts 1974 edn re Berwick C19/mid.

bear – barley... with six (or four) rows of grain on its ear, Heslop/Tyne 1880s; four-rowed barley, Brockett Nth C19/1. [OE bere].

big or **bigge** – the ancient name in the north for barley – from which the Bigg Market Newcastle is called, *Bell MS* C19/1; **bigg** – a coarse kind of barley; properly that variety which has six rows of grain on each ear, Brockett/Nth C19/1; barley esp. the four-rowed barley, Heslop/Tyne 1880s. [ON byggja].

bing – a chest in a stable to keep the horses corn in, *Bell MS* C19/1; **bin** or **bing** – a space or wooden receptacle for corn in a stable, Luckley/Alnwick 1870s. [ON bingr 'heap', Dan. bing 'bin'].

by-bootings – coarse flour, Bell MS C19/1. [?residue of bolting i.e. sieving].

caff – chaff, the husk of oats: 'a caff bed' Heslop/Tyne 1880s. [OE ceaf] (B)(H)(T).

chisel – bran, Bailey/Co. D'm 1810; chisel, **chizzel** – a common quality of meal from oats, Heslop/Tyne 1880s; **chisel** – a kind of bran with which boys feed rabbits, Palgrave/Hetton 1896. [OE ceosol].

choppy – pony feed: chopped hay or straw for fodder, Hull/wNewc 1880s; corn-like food for the pony, J.M./Dawdon 1970s. [chop] (H).

fad – 1 fad = 9 pounds [of wheat straw]. Robson N'd C19/2.

grey-stones – coarse mill stone... in oposition to the blue-stones, for finer meal, made of the whinstone, Brockett/Nth C19/1.

groats – shelled oats, Bailey/Co. D'm 1810. [ME grotan].

haver – oats [Northern] Kennet MS, 1695; **havermeal** – oatmeal, Heslop/Tyne 1880s, Dinsdale/Tees 1849. [ON hafre] (T: havel).

hinder-ends – refuse corn, *Bell MS* C19/1.

hummel – to 'shill' or take the outer cuticle off barley, Luckley/Alnwick 1870s; **humbling** barley – breaking off the awns (beards), with a flail or other instrument, Bailey/Co. D'm 1810. [source unknown].

kave – to separate with a rake and the foot the short straw from corn, Bailey/Co. D'm 1810. [cf. chave, chaff].

mang – barley or oats ground with the husk, for dogs and swine meat, Bailey/Co. D'm 1810; **mang** – to mix up, to intermingle {esp. food stuffs] Atkinson/Cleveland 1863. [OE gemengen 'mixed'].

pubble – plump, full: usually said of corn or grain when well perfected, Bailey/Co. D'm 1810. [Cf Fris. pumpel 'fat peson'].

snod – wheat ears are said to be 'snod' when they have no beards or awms [D'm] Kennet 1690s. [cf. ON snothinn 'bald'].

yaits (aits) – oats, Bailey/Co. D'm 1810; **aits, yaits, yetts** – oats, Brockett Nth C19/1. [OE átan (pl.)].

Butchers meat

braxy meat – from animal that died of natural causes, D.G., Hexhamshire.

camel – used to hang a lamb carcase up by the hocks to finish skinning after it had been opened up along the belly and inside back leg, D.G., Hexhamshire.

chitlins – intestines from chickens, etc. HP Cockfield C20. [source unknown].

colley – butcher's meat. A term chiefly among children, Brockett/Nth C19/1; butcher's meat (not bacon or salted meat) Heslop/Tyne 1880s. [ON kolla 'cow'].

an **ear** or a **niere** – a kidney, Bailey/Co. D'm 1810; 'the ear of veal' cf. German 'Niere', Brockett/Nth C19/1. [ME nére, ON nyra].

harrigauds – means entrails, *Bell MS* C19/1.

mairt – a cow or ox slaughtered a Martinmas and salted for winter store. 'The custom of salting meat to last throughout the inclement months was universal among our ancestors. Though less frequent, since the extensive cultivation of turnips, it still partially prevails in Northumberland...' Brockett/Nth C19/1; mairt / **mart** – a bullock bought by two or more persons – it was afterwards killed and divided amongst the purchasers, Heslop/Tyne 1880s. [Gael. mart 'cow, ox'].

painch-wife – tripe-seller, Heslop/Tyne 1880s. [paunch].

puddings. Intestines: 'A'll pull thy puddin's oot!' Palgrave/Hetton 1896. (Hence, Pigs'-puddings, Black-pudding.) [ME podyng 'stuffed entrails'].

saim – hog's lard, Luckley/Alnwick 1870s. [OFr saim].

traik – dead mutton as opposed to butchered mutton, Heslop/Tyne 1880s. [esp. Scots, source uncertain].

trolly-bags – a part of tripe, Heslop/Tyne 1880s; **trollibobs, trollibogs** – entrails: 'tripes and trollibobs' Atkinson/Cleveland 1863. [*OED* trillibubs – source unknown].

Milk products

aig – sourness: 'the milk has got an aig' Brockett/Nth C19/1. [OFr aigre].

beestings, beestlings – the first milk which a cow gives after her calving [Yorks] Kennet MS 1695; **beastlings** or **beastings** – the thick milk given by the cow for a short time after calving, Brockett/Nth C19/1. [OE bíesting] (B: milk from nearly calved cow).

blake – yellow, of a golden colour – spoken of butter, cheese, etc. Heslop/Tyne 1880s. [OE blác, ON bleikr 'pale'].

blashy – thin: 'poor blashy milk or beer' (Nb) Grose 1787. [imit.].

boily – properly, food prepared specially for an infant's use; milk with soft bread crumbled fine [and] boiled in it, Atkinson/Cleveland 1863; **boilee** – milk and bread and sugar, South Moor (Stanley) 2003; **boilie** – chunks of bread in a basin, with a few raisins mixed in for flavour and scalded with boiling water. Milk was added, if available, B.J., Newbottle C20/mid; crustless white bread scalded with hot water, drained, then milk added, Blenkin/Shildon C20/2. [Fr bouillie].

brat – the filmy skin on boiled milk, Bell MS C19/1. [OIrish brat 'cloth, covering'].

bull jumpings – a sort of custard made of beestlings and given to young folk (Hexham) Bell MS C19/1.

cracket – three-legged small (milking?) stool, Blenkin/Shildon C20/2. [cf. Du kruk 'stool'].

flaun – a custard baked in paste, Atkinson/Cleveland 1863. [source unknown].

kairn-milk – butter-milk, Heslop/Tyne 1880s. [churn].

keslop – the stomach of a calf, Grose 1787; a calf's stomach salted and dried to make rennet Bailey/Co. D'm 1810; **cheese-lop, cheslip, cheslop**, Atkinson/Cleveland 1863. [OE cése-lyb 'cheese-potion'].

kirn or kurn – a butter churn, *Bell MS* C19/1; **kyrne** – a churn (1479-80) Raine/Finchale; a kerne – a chern or churn, *Kennet MS*, 1695. [OE cyrin, ON kirna].

kirned – churned: 'an kirn'ed ed Fridays' Egglestone/Weardale C19/2; **kern** – to churn; a churn, Brockett/Nth C19/1.

lopper – to coagulate, Luckley/Alnwick 1870s; to curdle, Brockett/Nth C19/1; **loppered-milk** – sour curdled milk, Grose 1787. [ON hloypa 'to curdle']; **loppered-milk** – "milk turned sour was either loppered or bratty", N'd ca.1950 per F.W.

meal of milk – as much as a cow gives at one milking, Bailey/Co. D'm 1810.

strippings – the last part of a cow's meal, said to be richer than the rest, Bailey/Co. D'm 1810.

to bishop – to let milk or sauce burn… in boiling, *Bell MS* C19/1 ['because the bishops burn who they lust and whosoever displeaseth them' – Tindale].

Fruits

barries – berries. Generic name for all fruit of the berry kind, Palgrave/Hetton 1896; **berries** – gooseberries, par excellence, Atkinson/Cleveland 1863.

blackbarries – blackberries Dobson 7; blackberries – blackcurrants, Atkinson/Cleveland.

black bow-wowers – bramble berries (N'd) *Bell MS* C19/1; plus **bumbly kites** Luckley/Alnwick 1870s.1863.

blae-berry – the bilberry or whortleberry, Heslop/Tyne 1880s; **blea-berry, blay-berry** – the bilberry or black whortle berry, Brockett/Nth C19/1; **bleeberry** (blae:beri) bilberry. 'The /e/ in 'berry' is quite distinct in compounds in the dialect, never as in literary English ('blea-berry,' not 'bleab'ry')' Palgrave/Hetton 1896. [ON blá 'blue, livid'].

brambles – blackberries (the fruit, not the plant) Blenkin/Shildon C20/2; brambles (always) – blackberry bushes and their fruit. Blackberry jam is always 'bramble jam.' 'Apple and bramble tart,' 'Bramble pudding' (from a menu at the North of England Café, Durham) Palgrave/Hetton 1896. [OE brembel].

bumblekites – bramble berries (fruit of *Rubus fructicosus*) Bailey/Co. D'm 1810; **bummlekite, bummlerskite** – the blackberry, the fruit of the bramble, Heslop/Tyne 1880s. [affects the 'kite' or belly].

bunch-berry – the fruit of the *Rubus saxatilis*, Brockett, Nth C19/1.

caller – cool, refreshing: 'Caller ripe grosers' Brockett/Nth C19/1. [?Sco. calver].

carberries – gooseberries, Atkinson/Cleveland 1863. [source unknown].

cattijugs – hips, the fruit of the cat-whin or dog-rose, Atkinson/Cleveland 1863.

choup, cat-choup – a hip; the fruit of the hedge briar or wild rose, Brockett/Nth C19/1; **choups** – heps [sic], the fruit of briars, Bailey/Co. D'm 1810. [choup = hip, cf. Norw. kjupa].

cloud-berry – the ground mulberry or *Rubus chamæmorus*, Brockett Nth C19/1; also **noops, knot-berry, knout-berry**, Heslop/Tyne 1880s.

craw-crooks – the crow-berry, Brockett/Nth C19/1. [properly *Empetrum nigrum*].

curranberries – red currants, Heslop/Tyne 1880s; **curn-berries** – currants, Brockett Nth C19/1; **curran** or **corran barries** – garden currants black and red, Hull/wNewc 1880s; **corn-barries** – red or white currants, Heslop/Tyne 1880s. [Corinth].

feg – 'the name invariably given by the vulgar to fig' Brockett/Nth C19/1.

gean tree – the wild cherry, Heslop/Tyne 1880s. [Fr guine, guigne].

goosegob – gooseberry, Blenkin/Shildon C20/2.

goosegog – gooseberry, HP Cockfield C20; goosegogs, RM Norton C20/mid.

grosers – 'goose-berries or grozers' W. Lawson *New Orchard & Garden* ca. 1648 per Raine MS; grosers – gooseberries, Bailey/Co. D'm 1810; 'to jump like a cock at a grozer'. Heslop/Tyne 1880s; 'berries en grozers' Egglestone/Weardale C19/2. [Fr groseille].

heck-berry – sloe, Dinsdale/Tees 1849. [hackberry, *Prunus padus*; cf. ON heggr].

hindberries – raspberries (*Rubus Idæus*) Bailey/Co. D'm 1810. [OE hindberie].

hoggins, wicks, wickens – words used to describe blackberries in abundance, Sanderson/Easington 1950s.

horse-gogs – a fair-sized but highly astringent blue plum, Atkinson/Cleveland 1863.

knoop – the cloudberry, Brockett/Nth C19/1; noops, knupes – the fruit of the cloudberry, Heslop/Tyne 1880s.

knoutberry – a dwarf mulberry, Brockett/Nth C19/1.

ploted – well plucked, of a blackberry bush, Easington Colliery 2001. [Flem/Du ploten].

puzzin berries – the red berries of the mountain ash, Luckley/Alnwick 1870s. [poison].

rasp – raspberry, Grose 1787; both the bush and its fruit, Brockett/Nth C19/1. [source unknown].

scrab – a wild apple, the crab, Brockett/Nth C19/1; scrabes – crab apples, Cuth. Fair C16. [cf Swed. skrabba].

slae / slay – the sloe: 'slay bus' (a sloe bush) Heslop/Tyne 1880s. [OE slá, *Prunus spinosa*].

spice – dried fruit. Hence, spice-cake, a cake full of currants, Brockett/Nth C19/1.

wind-berry – billberry or whortleberry, Ray/North 1673; a wind-berry – a whortle-berry or bill-berry [Northern] *Kennet MS* 1695. [winberry, OE wínberie].

wyeberries – the fruit of the red whortleberry (wine-berry) Heslop/Tyne 1880s.

Other wild food

arnut / yarnut – earth nut, Bailey/Co. D'm 1810. [*Bunium flexiosum*].

brown-lemur – a ripe brown hazel-nut that readily separates from its husk, Brockett/Nth C19/1.

fusba' – fuzzball, a fungus… a puff-ball, Brockett Nth C19/1; **fuz-ball** – a fungus (the puffball) Dinsdale/Tees 1849; **fuzz-ball** – a species of fungus, Grose 1787. [*Lycoperdon bovista*].

leam – of a hazel nut, when it becomes brown or ripe: 'it leams well' Brockett/Nth C19/1. [leam 'the husk of nut'].

lemurs – ripe nuts that separate easily from the husk, Bailey/Co. D'm 1810.

runch – a general name for wild mustard, white mustard and wild radish, Bailey/Co. D'm 1810; the wild mustard plant, Atkinson/Cleveland 1863; wild mustard, charlock, Brockett/Nth C19/1. [source unknown].

yellows – the runch or wild mustard amongst the corn, Bell MS C19/1.

Vegetables

ackersprit – the premature sprouting of a potato, the germination of grain, Brockett/Nth C19/1. [techn. from Gk].

cabbish – cabbage, Egglestone/Weardale C19/2.

casket – cabbage-stalk, Palgrave/Hetton 1896; **castock** – the stem of a cabbage. Robson N'd C19/2 [source unknown].

finkle – the plant fennel, Brockett/Nth C19/1. [ME fenecel, Du venkel].

howk – to dig up, to excavate: 'are ye on howkin taties?' Heslop/Tyne 1880s. [nME holk, cf. OE holc 'cavity'].

kail – cabbage, greens, Brockett/Nth C19/1; **cale** – cabbage: 'cale plants' 1526 via Yk Raine MS. [ON kál, OE cól].

maumy – mellow and [juicy] Bailey/Co. D'm 1810; **maum** – mellow, possessing the softness of maturity or ripeness, Atkinson/Cleveland 1863. [OE mealm–, ON malmr].

pig taties – soft potatoes unfit for human consumption, used as pig feed. Norman Wilson, Newburn.

scallion – spring onions, Blenkin/Shildon C20/2; a young onion, before the bulb has formed. A favourite dish is scallion and lettuce, Palgrave/Hetton 1896. [AF scaloun].

shaw – the green top of stalk of a plant: 'tatie shaw', 'neep shaw' Heslop/Tyne 1880s; the haulm or leafy stalk of potatoes, Luckley/Alnwick 1870s. [source unknown].

tatie-boggle – a scarecrow, Heslop/Tyne 1880s; **tattie boggle**, Newc. 2001.

tatie-pie – potato clamp (heap of potatoes covered in straw then earth, for storage) Blenkin/Shildon C20/2.

taties – potatoes, Wilson/G'head 1820s; **tatties**, Barnard Castle 2001; **chyetties** Tyneside. 2001; **tetty**: 'tetty-flavoured crisps' Dobson 7; **chetties**, Thornley 2001.

Turnip

bagie – turnip Dobson 1/8; bagie (a as in day, the g hard) – a Swede turnip… never applied to white or yellow turnips, Heslop/Tyne 1880s. [Swed. rutabaga].

barebacks – turnips with the tops cut off, Heslop/Tyne 1880s.

fosey / phosey – frost bitten [re] turnips, Heslop/Tyne 1880s [see also 'bad food'] [cf. Du voos, Norw. fos 'spongey'].

narky – S'd, Southwick 2001; term for sweet white turnip. Silksworth.

nammies – Phillips/Cullercoats.

nasher – "because animals gnash it" SM Ho'ton/Penshaw, CT New Herrington, Houghton C20/2.

nashy – S'd. 2001.

neep – a turnip: "hoeing neeps" Heslop/Tyne 1880s. [OE naep].

snadger – Tyneside, Winlaton, South Shields. Birtley, Cleadon Park 2003.

snadgie – Tyneside 2001.

snagger – "when too frosty to pull [turnip] out by top, you stick the point of the snagger in to get a grip, then the main blade for topping and tailing. Hand harvesting continued until about 1990; every farm would have turnips as a crop" SM Ho'ton/Penshaw C20/2; South Moor (Stanley) 2003, Thornaby, Saltburn, Wear Valley, B'p Auckland, H'pool, Lanchester 2001; "My friend fron Horden knew the orange one as a Snagger" (E), Belmont 2006; snaggers – "definitely at Easington Colliery for turnip. A Halloween lamp made from one was a maggie as in 'Jack shine yor maggie'. The stench of smoked, charred and burnt turnip was aarful…" Sanderson/Easington 1950s; **go snagging turnips** – to chop off the leaves, HP Cockfield C20.

snanny – Gateshead 2001; Seaton Burn, Coxhoe, Gosforth, Gateshead, Dinnington, Winlaton C20/mid.

snarter – Seaham C29/2 [cf. ON snarr, snart 'severe, sharp'].

snasha – turnip *Dodd MS*, Tanfield Lea C20/2, CT New Herrington.

swill – hazel or wire oval basket for carrying mainly chopped turnips, D.G., Hexhamshire.

tormit – a turnip; **tormit shaw** – a turnip top, Heslop/Tyne 1880s; **tormit** – turnip, Luckley/Alnwick 1870s; tormit or **turmit** – a common pronunciation of turnip Brockett/Nth C19/1.

tunger – Shotton Colliery, Middlesbrough.

tungie – H'pool per VW C20/2; tungy M'bro. 2001, tunjy Whatley Hill; **tungie-snackin'** – (harvesting) M'bro per VW C20/2.

tunnip snaggin' – harvesting, Saltburn, Cleveland C20/2 per VW.

turnep –turnip or swede, Blenkin/Shildon C20/2.

yammy – S'd. 2001.

Pease

blendings or **blendlings** – a mixture of peas and beans, Brockett Nth C19/1.

brandlings – large peas of a brownish yellow spotted colour, quite different from the ordinary grey peas, much fancied and in request for 'carlins', Heslop/Tyne 1880s. [re variegated colour].

brusle – to dry: 'brustled pease' (Nb) French 'brusler', Grose 1787. [?Fr brusler 'to burn'].

carlings – see Food Ceremonies.

haulm – the stalk of pease, beans, etc. Luckley/Alnwick 1870s. [OE healm 'stem'].

peas – "Could mak a meal of a piece of tarry towt 'n' a tin o peas" (anon.) Silksworth.

pea-swad – a pea-shell, pod, Heslop/Tyne 1880s; pea swabs – peapods. Norman Wilson, Newburn.

scadded peas – green grey peas baked in their swads or peascods, *Bell MS* C19/1. [scald].

scadding of peas – a custom in the North of boiling the common grey-peas in their shell, Grose 1787.

shill – to separate, to shell, Atkinson/Cleveland 1863; **shill, sheal, shell** [to shell or dehusk] peas or oats, Heslop/Tyne 1880s.

skeel – to shell, Heslop/Tyne 1880s. [?scale – OFr escaler].

swad – a pod: 'a pea-swod, a bean-swad' Heslop/Tyne 1880s. [source uncertain].

2. The kitchen

The fire and its furniture

alow (ow like ou in trout) – ablaze, alight: 'it wis aall iv alow iv a minute' Heslop/Tyne 1880s.

amers – cinders from the oven, *Bell MS* C19/1. [source unknown].

andirons – irons on the hearth to support burning wood, Heslop/Tyne 1880s. [OFr andier].

backstone – a flat stone used for baking oatcakes, etc. 'The bakstone was often 3 or 4 ft in diameter, capable of holding 2 cakes, and fixed upon 3 or 4 pillars; the girdle was less and lighter, and upon an iron tripod, called a brandreth' Hodgson *Northumberland* pt.2, vol.2, p.306 n. per p.31 Heslop/Tyne 1880s; **backstone** – a heated stone for baking unleavened cakes upon, before iron plates were used... Stones are still in use for oatcakes, Brockett Nth C19/1; In Wales and the Pennines, flat oatcakes were baked on a bakestone, a heated stone slab placed on the hearth, *Eveleigh* p.28; **backstan** – a sheet of iron, sometimes a stone having an iron hoop to enable it to be hung over the fire, used to bake cakes upon, Staithes 1930 (plus **backstan-ceeak**) [bake than back].

bake stick – a wooden contrivance somewhat like a painters easel, used in Northumberland to place a girdle cake in front of the fire, Bell MS C19/1; **back-sticks**, bake-sticks – a triangular frame of wood or iron, resembling a small easel, with a prop at the back, for holding girdle cakes in front of the fire to finish the baking, or sometimes to warm an old cake, Heslop/Tyne 1880s.

bleezer – a sheet of iron for closing the open space above a grate to increase the draught, Hull/wNewc 1880s; **blazer** – a piece of sheet iron, put between the grate and the mouth of the chimney, in order to make the fire draw, Palgrave/Hetton 1896; 'put the bleezer up, and let's hev a lowe' Heslop/Tyne 1880s; **bleezer** – a sheet of tin with a handle in the centre... popped up to restrict air entry up the chimney and force the air to come through the fire from underneath the burning coal, HP.

brand-irons / and-irons – the irons for holding up the logs in a wood fire, Heslop/Tyne 1880s.

brandreth – the beam across the kitchen chimney from which the reckon-crook hangs. Also the beam for a well on which the rope coils: 'ye brendreth in ye kitchen chimney' Dishforth, Norton, 1672 Raine MS; **brandrith** – a trivet, Ray via Heslop/Tyne 1880s; **brandaret** – tripod for cooking over a fire (1465) Raine/Finchale. [ON brand-reith 'a grate'].

briggs – an iron set over fire: 'a paire of brigges to set a pan on over the fier' Walton, 1624 Raine MS. [bridge].

brochys – spits (1465) Raine/Finchale. [OFr broche 'pin, broach'].

cake-creel – a rack at the top of a kitchen to dry oatcakes, Brockett via Heslop/Tyne 1880s. [cf OFr greille 'wicker-work'].

cauldron – "cauldrons were round bellied and round bottomed and by the middle ages were being made with three legs which gave them stability and enabled the to stand in the fire." *Eveleigh* p.15 [made of cast metal] [AF caud(e)ron, Fr chaud(e)ron].

clypes – pot hooks (1354) Raine/Finchale. [from vb OE clyppan, ON klypa].

dog – "a metal plug for the fireback, it covered the hole in the back of the fire – when removed the fire would 'draw' and so heat the side oven" Teward/Teesdale C20/mid; 'dog' was piece of iron, often with 4 or 5 holes, acting as a damper between fire and oven flues, and permitted some regulation of oven heat, Silksworth. ['dog' applied to any mechanical fastening or grip]

dutch oven – introduced in the eighteenth century… 'they were made of tinplate and stood in front of the fire, the bright surface reflecting the heat, reducing cooking time and saving fuel.' *Eveleigh* p.21. [First mentioned in print in Dickens *David Copperfield* (1849) ch. 24: 'I'll toast you some bacon in a bachelor's Dutch-oven that I have got here.'].

fire-cods – bellows, Atkinson/Cleveland 1863. [ON koddi, 'pillow', OE cod 'bag'].

flaik, flake – a wooden frame at the top of a kitchen for keeping oatcakes upon, Brockett Nth C19/1. [ON flake 'frame'].

galley-baak – the balk or beam fixed across a chimney over the fire, from which a pot hook called a 'reetin cruch' was hung. The galley-baak was sometimes a tree branch with the bark stripped off, but otherwise undressed and unsquared. In this case it was commonly called a 'peeled grain, Helsop/Tyne 1880s [ON bálkr 'beam'].

hud – the side, or rather the covering of the top of the side, of a fireplace, Brockett/Nth C19/1. [confusion with nook, below?].

ingle – a fire or blaze [Cumb'land] Ray/North 1673; fire or flame, Grose 1787; fire, flame; fireside, Atkinson/Cleveland 1863. [?Gael. aingeal 'fire, light'].

izle – a live ember of wood, the embers of a fire, Heslop/Tyne 1880s. [OE ysel 'spark, ember', ON usli 'fire'].

keggins – fireside hooks to hang pans on, Teward/Teesdale C20/mid. [source unknown].

lowe – flame, vb. to flame, Ray/North 1673; 'to make a lowe' – to stir the fire in order to make it blaze, Grose 1787; low – to flame in Yorksh, as the fire lows… **low** – flame, fire [Northern]… lowe in the North – the flame of fire, Kennet MS 1695. [ON loge].

lum – the chimney of a cottage, Brockett/Nth C19/1; lum – a chimney ('so called in Newcastle') *Raine MS*; a **loom** or **lumm** – a chimney [D'm] *Kennet MS* 1695. [cf. OFr lum 'light', OWelsh 'llumon 'chimney'].

need-fire – fire obtained by rubbing two pieces of dry wood together, Heslop/Tyne 1880s. [OE nied-fyr, Norw naudeld].

nook or **nuke** – a corner: 'laye in a newke nigh the fier' Ebchester, 1526 via D'm *Raine MS* [source uncertain; compare: hood or hud as space at back or side of fireplace first mentioned 1641 (*OED*)].

pot-cleps / pot-kelps – pot-hooks, or hooks used for suspending pots over the kitchen fire. Heslop/Tyne 1880s.

a **racken** or **racen** – pot-hangers in Yorkshire; in the bishoprick of Durham a **racen-crouk**, Kennet MS 1695; **reckans** – hooks for pots over fires Ray/North 1673+; **rackan / rackan-cruk / rackin-cruck** – a pot-hook or chain and hook for suspending pots over a fire, Heslop/Tyne 1880s; **recken-cruck** – a crook hung on a bar in the chimney of most country houses, on which they hung the kale-pot on, Bell MS C19/1; **wrekins** – a steel bar hooked at both ends, one end to go over the rannel bork bar… the other end to hook pans or kettles on, Teward/Teesdale C20/mid. [OE racente, ON rekendi 'chain'].

rakynt' – a reckin tree, a horizontal bar of wood or iron, placed at a suitable height in the reek or smoke of a chimney, from which vessels are suspended over the fire, Raine/Finchale C15.

rannel bork – the cross bar on an old fireplace… from it hung the reckins, Teward/Teesdale C20/mid; **rannel bauk** – chimney cross-beam, *Moorman Yorks* 1678. [Cf Norw rand-tre].

reed – the pronunciation of red: 'reedhet' Heslop/Tyne 1880s. [OE réad].

reek – smoak, *Bell MS* C19/1; 'chimley reek', 'baccy reek' Heslop/Tyne 1880s; 'reeking hot' Grose 1787; **reeky** – smoky Atkinson/Cleveland 1863. [OE réc, ON reykr].

reek – to emit smoke: 'the chimley's reekin badly' Heslop/Tyne 1880s.

reek penny – a petty tithe paid by every house in which a fire was burned: 'a reeke Penny of every inhabitant keeping house' Hamsterley, 1629 via D'm, Raine MS.

rozzel / rosel / rosin – to warm [e.g. at a fire]: 'rosel yor shins' Heslop/Tyne 1880s.

salamander – a poker with a flat, thickened end, heated red-hot in the fire, for thrusting into an unlighted fire, Palgrave/Hetton 1896. [re legend of fiery salamander].

sooker – an iron plate fitted to an old fashioned kitchen range to restrict the flue opening, F.W., Annfield Plain.

spink – a spark of fire or light, Brockett/Nth C19/1; a spink of fire – a spark [D'm] *Kennet MS* 1695. [source uncertain].

stove – gas stove, etc. C19. [MDu stove 'heated room'].

swale, sweal – to singe or burn, to waste or blaze away, Ray/North 1673. [OE swælan 'to burn'].

tidy betty – a short fender across the grate, without a bottom, Palgrave/Hetton 1896.

tidy – stand with brush, rake and tongs, CT New Herrington C20/mid.

trivet – 'a stand for a pot, kettle, or other vessel placed over a fire for cooking or heating something: orig. and properly standing on three feet' OED; 'A gyrdle, a brandrett, a speitt, and a trippet' Richmond Wills 1563 *Raine MS*.

winter – the bracket hooked on to the bars of a grate, upon which anything may be heated in front of the fire, Palgrave/Hetton 1896; **winter/ wunter** – an iron frame made to fit on the bars of the kitchen range, on which sad-irons are placed to be heated. It is also used for heating or cooking anything before the bars of the fire, Heslop/Tyne 1880s. [source uncertain].

yoon – oven Ray/North 1673+; **yown, yune** – an oven, Atkinson/Cleveland 1863; **yuven** – an oven, Heslop/Tyne 1880s, Tanfield Lea C19/2; **eeavun** – oven, Staithes 1930 ('Yuon' generally in Cleveland.) [OE ofn, ON ofn].

Fuel

bath brick – used to clean and polish steel fenders, and cutlery, Crocker/Spennymoor C20/1.

beet – to help or assist… 'To beet the fire' – to feed it with fuel… straw, heath, fern, furze, and especially the husks of oats, when used for heating girdles on which oaten cakes are baked, Brockett Nth C19/1. [OE bétan 'to amend'].

to **brian** an oven – keep it alight by a fire at the mouth of it (Nb) Grose 1787. [source unknown].

buntin – the cone of the fir tree, Heslop/Tyne 1880s. [source unknown].

carbones maritimi – sea-coal, so called for being carried coast-wise (1358–9) Raine/Finchale.

casings – dry cow dung used as fuel: 'one mow of casens wt some other fewell' Gt Driffield, 1679 Raine MS; **cassons** Usburne, 1602/03 *Raine MS*; **cassings, cassons, cow-blakes** – cow dung dried in the sun for fuel, Brockett Nth C19/1. [var. of casing].

cats – coal dust mixed with clay, etc., and formed into balls for domestic heating (JG). [?cat as name of ball in game of tip-cat].

cat-whin – burnet gorse, Heslop/Tyne 1880s.

chats, chatts – cones of the fir-tree, Atkinson/Cleveland 1863. [Fr chats, applied to various seeds, etc.].

clog – a log, block of wood, Atkinson/Cleveland 1863; 'put a clog on the fire' Luckley/Alnwick 1870s. [source unknown].

cow-blakes – cow-dung [for fuel] Ray/North 1673.

dolly muck – a very fine coal dust used to bank up fires overnight, Crocker/Spennymoor C20/1. [?dolly for dowly].

duff (doof) – fine coal, or coal dust (the only name in use). Hence, duffy, trashy, cheap and nasty (of sugar)… Palgrave/Hetton 1896. [probably from duff as 'worthless'].

eldin' – fuel for a fire, Atkinson/Cleveland 1863; eldin – firewood, Dinsdale/Tees 1849; eldin, elding – fuel, such as turf, peat, or wood, Brockett Nth C19/1. [ON elding].

fir-apple – fir-cone, Dinsdale/Tees 1849.

glede, gleed – a coal in a state of strong heat, Brockett Nth C19/1. [OE gléd 'anything burning red-hot'].

ling – heath (*Erica vulgaris*) Bailey/Co. D'm 1810; the heather of the moors, Atkinson/Cleveland 1863. [Properly *Caluna vulgaris*, RO, Wooler] [ON lyng].

scrab apples – fir cones, Luckley/Alnwick 1870s.

sea-coal – 1. coal gathered on the seashore.
  2. the mineral coal, as opposed to other fuels in combustion (wood, charcoal).
  3. coal shipped by sea.
  4. coal reserves under the sea.

spales or **spyalls** – refuse chips for firing, Bell MS C19/1; **spile / spail** (Nth N'd) / **speal / spyel** (Sth N'd) – a wooden pike, a splinter of wood, chips from an axe-cut: 'aa's just getten a few spyels for the mornin's fire' Heslop/Tyne 1880s. [cf Norw spela].

whins – gorse or furze: 'whinns, for baking' (expenses, Sherburn Hospital, 1686) Brockett/Nth C19/1; 'xiii loods of furres or whynnes' Castle Eden 1576/77 via Durham, *Raine MS*; **whuns** – furze or gorse: 'whuns on the moor' Luckley/Alnwick 1870s. [cf. Dan. hvine].

Cooking utensils

batty tins – tins for cooking a group of individual cakelets, Teward/Teesdale C20/mid.

bill-knife – a knife used by butchers for cracking bones, Palgrave/Hetton 1896. [OE bil 'sword'].

girdle – a circular iron plate, with a bow handle, on which thin and broad cakes of bread are baked, Brockett Nth C19/1; **girdle / gordle** – Heslop/Tyne 1880s; **griddles** or girdles... thick circular plates of iron, usually about 12 inches diameter *Eveleigh* p.28. [AF grédil 'gridiron'].

gully – a large sharp knife used in farm-houses, principally to cut bread, cheese, etc., for the family; also used by butchers in killing sheep, Brockett/Nth C19/1; **gully** – beadknife. Dinsdale/Tees 1849; a common hous-knife, *Kennet MS*, 1695; gully – 'used by the fish man who came to the door; it had a unique shape' Sanderson/Easington 1950s. [source unknown].

haveridils – riddles for haver or oats (1479–80) Raine/Finchale [haver + riddle].

kail-pot – a crock to boil cabbage (kail), etc. in, Palgrave/Hetton 1896; large metal cooking pot, Dinsdale/Tees 1849; kale-pot – a pottage-pot... a large semi-globular, full-bottomed iron pot on three spiky legs, Atkinson/Cleveland 1863; 'the kail-pot's callin' the yetlin' smutty' (saying).

keling-fatt – a cooking [vessel]: 'ii kelyng fattes' Sherburn in Elmet, 1437/38 *Raine MS*. [OE célan, ON koela 'to cool'].

kettle – cooking utensil made from sheet metal, e.g. brass, later copper or tin plate – for boiling water, cooking fish in water, etc. Open top fitted with lid. *Eveleigh* p.19 [source: Old English kytel].

piggin – a iron pot with two ears, also a wooden pot with a handle, *Bell MS* C19/1. [source unknown].

pirtle – a short stick used for stirring porridge, Heslop/Tyne 1880s. [source unknown].

riddle – a sieve. Various dialects, Palgrave/Hetton 1896. [late OE hriddel].

sile – a strainer, Atkinson/Cleveland 1863; a sieve, Upper Teesdale 2001. [ON síle].

skillet – metal pan with long handle and three stubby legs, *Eveleigh* p.19; **skellet** – saucepan, Staithes 1930. [cf. OFr esculette 'small plate'].

spurtle – a cake turner made of wood with a handle on one end. The other end is tapered to a fine edge, F.W., Annfield Plain.

temse – a sieve made of hair, used in the dressing of flour, Atkinson/Cleveland 1863; **tempse** – a fine cloth or silk sieve, Bell MS C19/1. [OE temese].

thivel – a smooth stick... especially for stirring hasty pudding, Brockett/Nth C19/1; **thybel** – a round stick, usually of willow... to stir porridge, Heslop/Tyne 1880s; thivel – a wooden stick for stirring with, e.g. cream before churning it into butter, Teward/Teesdale C20/mid. [source unknown] OE thyfe 'a bush, a branch'l.

yetlin' – pot: "away he gans te the fire an' lifts off the yetlin' boilin' an' steamin'" Haldane/Tyne 1890s; **yetlin / yetelin** – a small cast-iron pot with a rounded bottom... a miniature kail-pot, Heslop/Tyne 1880s; **yettlin** – a hemispherical metal pot with three legs and a bow handle, much used for boiling porridge and potatoes, Luckley/Alnwick 1870s; **yetlings** pro fixis – frying pans for fish (1411) Raine/Finchale; "**yettling** – a gypsy pot" Robson N'd C19/2. [OE geotan 'to pour']

Tubs and containers

ark – a large chest or coffer in farm houses, used for keeping corn or meal, Brockett/Nth C19/1. [OE arc, ON örc].

bait-poke – a bag in which a pit-lad carries his provisions: 'Aw put the bait-poke on at eight', Wilson/G'head 1820s; a bate poke is what a workman carries his dinner or corn for his horses [in], *Bell MS* C19/1. [cf. ONF poque, OE pocca, Ice. poki, Gael. poca 'bag'].

cawel – 'a basket in the North, hence a cawel is a chicken-coop' [D'm] *Kennet MS*, 1695. [OE cawl 'basket'].

creel – fish basket; 'tipple your creels' – somersault, Blenkin/Shildon C20/2; **creel** – basket for wool, Dinsdale/Tees 1849; **creil** or creel – a kind of semi-circular basket of wicker work, in which provender is carried to sheep in remote pastures, Brockett/Nth C19/1. [cf OFr greille 'wicker-work'].

coop, coup – a vessel of wood, possibly made with staves, Atkinson/Cleveland 1863. [cf. Du kuip 'cask'].

a gowpen – as much as your hands will hold: 'a gowpen of meal' as an alms to the poor, also 'a gowpen of herbs' in medical prescriptions, *Bell MS* C19/1; **gowpen** – the hollow of both hands placed together: 'a gowpen o' yetts' Heslop/Tyne 1880s. [ON gaupn].

guisen (gaa:yzn) – to become dried and contracted, of rain-tubs or wooden cisterns, so that the water 'sipes' out. 'Yon tub'll guisen.' Palgrave/Hetton 1896; **guizend** – of tubs or barrels that leak through drought, Grose 1787. [ON gisna].

a kimmel – a poudring tub, Ray/North 1673. [ME kimnel].

kit – a milking pail, like a churn, with two ears and a cover, Grose 1787; properly a covered milking pail with two handles, but often applied to a small pail of any sort, Brockett/Nth C19/1. **band-kitt** – a sort of great can with a cover (Nb) Grose 1787. [MDu. kitte].

mug – a pot, a jar: 'a moug to put tar in' D'm Grassmen's Book, *Raine MS*. [cf. Norw. Mugge 'jug'].

piggin – a wooden cylindrical porringer, made with staves, and bound with hoops like a pail; holds about a pint, Bailey/Co. D'm 1810. [source unknown].

quaighs – a wooden cup composed of staves hooped together, *Bell MS* C19/1. [Gael. cuach 'cup'].

sipings – the drainings of a vessel after any fluid has been poured out of it, Bailey/Co. D'm 1810. [OE sipian (vb)].

skeel – a cylindrical wooden tub or vessel for carrying milk or water, Brockett/Nth C19/1; a cylindrical milking pail, with a handle made by one of the staves being a little longer than the rest, Bailey/Co. D'm 1810; **skeel** – a peculiarly-shaped bucket (broader at bottom than top, with upright stave projecting from rim, to serve as a handle), formerly used in colliery villages to carry water for household use. They were carried on women's heads on a 'wase', and a piece of wood was made to float on the top, to prevent the water from splashing over, Palgrave/Hetton 1896. [ON skjóla 'pail'].

skep – a hive for bees, also measure for corn, etc. *Bell MS* C19/1; **skepe** – a basket... made of whicker work or rushes (1397) Raine/Finchale; 'thre skeppes or baskettes with ote meal' Knaresborough, 1567/68 *Raine MS* [ON skeppa 'basket'].

so, soa – tub with two ears, to carry on a stang, Ray/North 1673+. [ON sár 'large tub'].

swill – a round basket of unpeeled willows, Brockett/Nth C19/1; **swill / sweel / swull** (Nth N'd) – a large open basket for carrying clothes, potatoes, etc. Heslop/Tyne 1880s [source unknown].

tommy box – for carrying food to work, Teesside steelworks 2001.

Processes

bolt – to teamse [to sift] *Bell MS* C19/1. [OFr bulter 'to pass meal through a bolting-cloth'].

bray – to beat, to pound, to reduce to powder, Brockett/Nth C19/1; 'braysyn mortar... to braye his spice in' Osbaldwicke, 1557 York via *Raine MS*. [OFr breier].

brissel – to scorch or dry very hard with fire, Bailey/Co. D'm 1810; **brizzle, bristle, birsel** – to crackle in cooking, Heslop/Tyne 1880s. [cf. Fr brusler 'to burn'].

coddle – to boil anything to meer pulp, as coddled grozers (gooseberry fool) *Bell MS* C19/1. [C16 only; source unknown – cf. quaddle, below].

dishclowt – dish cloth for washing up, Sterling/H'pool C20.

to drawk – to draggle, to mix as water and flower in kneading it, *Bell MS* C19/1. [ON drekkja 'to drench'].

"droon the miller" – If you put too much water in the bread or pastry mix and made it too 'claggy' (sticky) to roll out you had drowned the miller and had to add more flour to get the right consistency. Oxley/High Thornley.

graith – to furnish, provide or equip: 'bonnily graithed', 'a well graithed table' Atkinson/Cleveland 1863. [ON greitha].

jaup – shake any liquid, Dinsdale/Tees 1849; to agitate water or other fluid sharply in a vessel; to move as the shaken water in the vessel does, Atkinson/Cleveland 1863. [imit?]

keukt – cooked (p.p.) Armstrong/Tanfield C20/2.

quaddle – to boil and bubble: 'the pot's wauddlin on the hud' Heslop/Tyne 1880s.

range – to rinse; [cf] rench, Brockett/Nth C19/1; 'range oot the skeel' Luckley/Alnwick 1870s; 'Range the pot out' Palgrave/Hetton 1896. [ON hræinsa 'to cleanse'].

red – to put in order, to right: 'ye shud red up yer place', 'red yor hair' Luckley/Alnwick 1870s; red / **rid** – to tidy, to set out in order: 'get the hearth red up' Heslop/Tyne 1880s. [ON rethja, Du redden].

rench – to rinse, Brockett/Nth C19/1. [ON hreinsa, OFr reincer].

scaddin hot – scalding hot. Oxley/High Thornley.

sind – to wash out, to rinse, Atkinson/Cleveland 1863; to wash out by rinsing: 'just sind oot the coffee pot, hinney' Heslop/Tyne 1880s. [source unknown].

steep – soak in water. You would steep bread to make crowdy for the hens... N. Wilson, Newburn.

storken – to congeal, Dinsdale/Tees 1849; **storkin** or storken – to grow stiff, as melted fat cooled again, Bailey/Co. D'm 1810. [ON storkna 'to congeal'].

strenkle – to sprinkle: 'strenkle a leapyt ov sugar on't' Bewick/Tyne 1790s. [cf. sprinkle].

swale, sweal – to singe or burn, as 'to sweal a hog' Grose 1787. [OE swaelan 'to burn up'].

temse – to sift, Brockett/Nth C19/1; to put through a sieve: 'corne afore it be temsed' Best's Farming Book 1641 p.103 via *Raine MS.* [OE temsian].

wrench / range – to rinse, Heslop/Tyne 1880s. [var. of rench].

3. Food

General

backshift dinner – '… many people call a big meal a backshift dinner. I guess because the time you got a decent dinner was when you were on backshift'. (D.N.)

bait – a lunch taken on the road, *Bell MS* Newc 1815; food taken by a pitman to his work, *Nicholson* 1880; food carried for work or travel *Dodd MS* Tanfield Lea C20/2; packed meal, sandwiches etc., to take to work, Blenkin/Shildon C20/2; "my 'bait' of bread and jam" p.62 Hitchin/Dawdon 1910s; 'bait' also implies a break, a rest; "always white bread used for miners' bait" Forest Hall, Newc. **bait tin.** HP Cockfield C20. [from Old Norse beita].

belly-timmer – food, Wilson/G'head; food; a suply of material for the belly or stomach, Atkinson/Cleveland 1863.

chack – a slight refreshment, taken in haste, Heslop/Tyne 1880s.

chuck – food, provisions, Palgrave/Hetton 1896.

fusin – nourishment, Bailey/Co. D'm 1810; fusin, **fuzzen** – nourishment, abundance, Brockett/Nth C19/1.

meat – food, e.g. rabbit meat – a lettuce, dandelions, etc. Blenkin/Shildon C20/2; food: 'they w'd ha' nee time ta ki'ak nice meat' Egglestone/Weardale C19/2; 'Give the hens their meat' Palgrave/Hetton 1896; **butcher meat** – red meat, specifically (A. K.) [Compare Old English *mete* 'food'].

menseful – careful, economical. Robson N'd C19/2.

scran – food, Wilson/G'head 1820s, Sterling / H'pool C20; provision, Dinsdale/Tees 1849; verb 'scran' e.g. 'scrannin' (bolting food), "I could scran me bait". [origin uncertain; perhaps Common Germanic 'scran' (bits and pieces) influenced by Dutch schranzen (to eat lustily)].

snak – light meal, *Dodd MS* Tanfield Lea C20/2.

snap – food taken to work (Yorks, Lancs); snap – snack (usually sandwiches) Briscoe/Geordie 2003.

Oatmeal products

bannock – a thick cake of oaten or barley meal, kneaded with water... baked in the embers and toasted over again on a girdle when wanted to be used, Brockett/Nth C19/1; a thick cake of oaten or barley meal kneaded with water, Heslop/Tyne 1880s; thick cake of oat, barley or pease meal, Briscoe 2003. [Gael. Bannach].

brautins – girdle cakes with cheese sandwiched between, Heslop/Tyne 1880s.

cold-lord – a boiled pudding made of oatmeal and suet, Heslop/Tyne 1880s.

chimins – the seeds or inner husks of oats, soaked 2 or 3 days in cold water to become a jelly, and then boiled in water or milk... used in C'd, N'd [and Scotland]. Heslop/Tyne 1880s.

crowdie – porridge, Dinsdale/Tees 1849; oatmeal and water mixed together and used with milk butter or the fat from off the pot when beef is boiled, the last is called fat crowdie, *Bell MS* C19/1; oatmeal porridge, made thick enough to turn out of the basin, like a pudding, when cooled, Atkinson/Cleveland 1863; **crowdy** – a Northumberland dish, made by filling a basin with oatmeal, and then pouring on boiling water; in Scotland 'brose', Heslop/Tyne 1880s; oatmeal and hot water mixed together: 'The crowdy is wor daily dish' Wilson/G'head 1820s; oatmeal and boiling water stirred together till thick, and then 'supped' with milk, treacle, dripping, or beer sweetened with sugar, Luckley/Alnwick 1870s. [cf. Ice groutr 'porridge'].

cruppy-dow – a cake made of oatmeal and fish (N'd) Heslop/Tyne 1880s.

fadges – a large flat loaf or bannock, commonly of barley-meal and baked among the ashes, *Jamieson, Scots Dictionary* 1802; a thick cake of an oval shape made of wheaten meal and water, and baked upon a girdle – a circular iron plate, with a bow handle, on which thin and broad cakes of bread are baked, Brockett, Nth C19/1; a small loaf of bread... near the Border, a fadge is an oval bannock, or scone, about 2 or 3 inches thick, made of pease meal, often with an admixture of bean meal, and fired very hard on a 'girdle', Heslop/Tyne 1880s; thick cakes, baked in an oven being too thick to bake on the fire, *Bell MS* C19/1. [origin uncertain, but note fad – 'a bundle... such as can be conveniently carried under the arm or in the hand' Heslop Tyne 1880s] – see also under Breads.

farl or **farrel** – an oatcake. (N'd, Halliwell) or a fourth part of same, Heslop/Tyne 1880s; 'thin quarter-circles or 'farls' made without yeast' *Allen* re Scotland. [from fardel, OE feortha dael 'fourth part'].

fizzer – a singing hinnie without spice, Brockett Nth C19/1. [imit.].

frumenty or **frumity** – a dish made of bruised wheat or barley, boiled with milk, and seasoned with sugar and spices, Brockett Nth C19/1. [OFr frumentée].

girdle-cake / gordle-keyek – a name for the cakes baked on a girdle, Heslop/Tyne 1880s; **girdle-cake** – thin household bread baked on a girdle, Brockett Nth C19/1.

gruel – 'water gruell with ginger and sugar' *Bell MS*, Newc 1830s. [OFr gruel].

hasty pudding – hasty pudding or porridge oatmeal mixed in boiling water and stirred on the fire till it be considerably thickened, Brockett Nth C19/1; 'the most usual breakfast is bread and milk, and in winter when the latter is scarce, hasty pudding or crowdy is substituted for it' Bailey Co. Durham 1810; 'Bella cowp'd the hyesty-pudding on her new goon' Luckley/Alnwick 1870s.

haver-bread, haver-cake – large, round, thin oaten cakes, baked on a gridle; Brockett/Nth C19/1. [source, Old Norse hafre].

ned kyek – a cake kneaded with butter, etc. Luckley/Alnwick 1870s; **knedde-cake** – a cake kneaded with butter and baked on the girdle, Brockett/Nth C19/1; **ned-cake, kned-cake** – cake kneaded with butter, dripping or lard and generally baked on the girdle, Heslop/Tyne 1880s; 'ned cyek is pastry, syem as yer wad use fer pies and the like rowld out about abowt half te three quarters of an inch cut into abowt fower inch squares baked, left to cool, sliced, buttered' GD. [knead than need] See also under Breads.

poddish – porridge, Dinsdale/Tees 1849. [Fr pottage].

sack-porrage – hasty-pudding or porridge oatmeal mixed in boiling water and stirred on the fire till it be considerably thinkened. In Durham it is poddish. 'Put on the poddish-pot' Brockett/Nth C19/1. [porrage/porridge < pottage].

skilly – oatmeal and water, Robson/Tyne 1849; soup (in jail) *Dodd MS*, Tanfield Lea C20/2. [skilligalee].

sowans / sowens – a dish made from the seeds or inner husks of oats, which are soaked in water till they begin to turn sour. The water is then strained off and they are steeped agin in fresh water. This process is repeated a third time, and then the sowens are boiled and ready to eat. Fish liquor with a little salt is often used in preparing this dish. It is common in Scotland, N'd, and Nth C'd' Heslop/Tyne 1880s. [Gael. Sughan 'juice'].

spice – the only name known for currant-cake. 'Cake' always means teacake, Palgrave/Hetton 1896; gingerbread, or the admixture of currants with any food, Heslop/Tyne 1880s. [Fr espice].

spice-cake – currant cake, Heslop/Tyne 1880s; **spice-cakes** – teacakes enriched with currants, Atkinson/Cleveland 1863; 'a good speyce suet keayk' Bewick/Tyne 1790s.

spicy-fizzer – a currant cake, Wilson/G'head 1820s.

stoury – oatmeal and beer warmed together with a little sugar added to it, *Bell MS* C19/1; **stoury** – water gruell with ginger and sugar, *Bell MS* C19/1.

tharf cake – a girdle cake made of flour and water, *Bell MS* C19/1; "they never gat owse better than thaaf keahyk" Bewick/Tyne 1790s; **tharf-kyek** – Upper. Teesdale; "cut into squares to eat" (B/d Castle); **thauf-cake** or tharf-cake – a cake made of unfermented dough – chiefly of rye and barley – rolled very thin and baked hard (for keeping), Brockett/Nth C19/1; **tharf-kyek**, etc. – 'an unleavened cake made of barley-flour and wheat-meal with milk' Heslop Tyne 1880s; 'they never gat owse better than thaaf keahyk' Bewick 1790s. [OE theorf, ON thjarfr 'unleavened'].

tough cake (tyoof kyak) – a water-cake, or white-cake, baked on the girdle. No currants used, Palgrave/Hetton 1896.

twadgers – small round gingerbread cakes, slightly flavoured with lemon, Atkinson/Cleveland 1863.

wig – a teacake, Palgrave/Hetton 1896; **curran wig** – teacakes, Teward/Teesdale C20/mid. [MDu wigge 'wedge-shaped cake'].

Yule-dough – see FOOD CEREMONIES.

Breads

backust – bakehouse, Staithes 1930.

barley bread – 'Aw wunna hev barley breed' Luckley/Alnwick 1870s.

barm – yeast; **barmpot** – daft, idiot, HP Cockfield C20; **barmpot** – crazy man Sterling / H'pool C20; **barm-cake** – idiot H'pool, Teesside, Wingate 2001. [OE beorma].

barm-cake – Oxnard/Hetton 1990s; **barm-cake** – large bread roll (BG, S'd, 2005).

baxter – a baker, Heslop/Tyne 1880s.

booley bread – a stottie, A. P., Newc C20/mid.

bouted-bread – bread made of wheat and rye (Nb) Grose 1787 [bolted = sieved, graded].

chisel – wheat bran, the characteristic component of the genuine Tyneside broon breed, Hull/wNewc 1880s. [OE ceosol].

chuck – our word for bread was 'chuck' – my Dad would say "Cut me a slice o' chuck" Merihein/Ashington.

cob – a thick amorphous cake or loaf of bread. It was usually made from the last piece of dough, Heslop/Tyne 1880s. [source unknown; 'cob' implies roundness].

cruttelly – crumbly. 'The bread's cruttelly', K.P., Bednell.

damper bread – "We used to cook an inedible monstrosity called a damper out of flour and water in the Scouts – I think it was fried in a pan" Dave Neville.

eany and light – of bread, when the interior has a glazed appearance and is full of holes, Heslop/Tyne 1880s.

fadge – a properly risen round loaf, stottie means flat one, South Moor (Stanley) 2003; a small flat loaf, or thick cake, Brockett Nth C19/1; round, domed loaf, Belmont 2006; name fadgies proper to traingle or division of round loaf – M'bro.; sim. but called 'wedge' for quarter stottie, G'head, Stockton. [fadge – a bundle; one that is short and thick in person, Atkinson/Cleveland 1863; fad – a bundle …such as can be conveniently carried under the arm or in the hand, Heslop/Tyne 1880s].

granny loaf – small malted loaf with fruit in it, Blenkin/Shildon C20/2.

haver-bread – oatmeal bread, Grose 1787; **havel breed** – oatbread, Teward/Teesdale C20/mid. [haver=oats].

lev'in – bread dough, Teward/Teesdale C20/mid. [Fr levain, 'raising'].

masselgem – a mixture of wheat and rye for household bread, maslin, Brockett/Nth C19/1; massilgam – maslin: wheat and rye ground together and generally baked with leven, *Bell MS* C19/1; **masslinjem**/masselgem – maslin, wheaten meal and rye meal mixed for brown bread, Heslop/Tyne 1880s. [OE maestling 'alloy'].

ned cake – 'Sometimes lard would be mixed into the dough to make ned cakes' p.20 Hitchin/Dawdon 1910s; knodden-cake – a kneaded i.e. yeast-based cake, Dinsdale/Tees 1849.

new cake – freshly baked dough not as fully risen as for bread (Newc); new cake, round like stotty but lighter, more like a fadge. G'head.

pikelet – crumpet, N'd C20/mid; mentioned esp. Stockton, M'bro. [Welsh *bara pyglyd* 'pitchy (i.e. dark?) bread']

spice loaf – a spice loaf is made of dough and mixed with raisins, currants, allspice, ginger and different other aromatics, Newcastle 1900.

stottie-cake – "Oven bottom cake is known as 'stotty cake' in mining villages" N'd, 1938; stotty cuak – usually made from surplus dough after bread making also the oven has sufficiently cooled, CT New Herrington 1930s; stotty-cake – flat loaves, oven-bottom bread Shields/Tyne 1974; stottee kyek – large flat loaf *Dodd MS* Tanfield Lea C20/2; "My granny used to call stottie cakes 'oven bottom cakes' which I suppose suggests where it was baked." *Anon.* Sheriff Hill; "the stottie cake you get today we used to call them fadges" Beamish 1998/4 Ernie Cheesman; "a stottie is stotted to flatten it"; stotty-bun Seaham 2002; egg stottie, etc. – quarter of a stottie cake, sliced and filled like a sandwich, Seaham 2005. [re bouncy texture; a 1930s word?].

tuffies – bread buns, Thornley 2001; **tufty buns** – small bread buns, T.M., Parkside 1950s.

yest – yeast used for baking. Yeast bags were often sewn in pitman's jackets to carry 'log ends' home to chop up for sticks, HP Cockfield C20. [OE gist].

yesty kyek – a cake made with yeast, Luckley/Alnwick 1870s; 'With the broth were slabs of yester cake – flat, circular pieces of dough baked with the loaves.' p.20 Hitchin/Dawdon 1910s; **yesty-stot** Belmont 2006.

Broth

broth – always plural in the North. 'Will you have some broth?' 'I will take a few, if they are good.' Brockett Nth C19/1. ['little few broth'… originally perhaps 'a few broes', the Scotch for broth, and taken in England for the plural, Brockett/Nth C19/1] [OE, ON broth 'boiled item'].

kail, kyel – broth or soup, especially when made with potatoes or fish: 'Will ye hev a few tatie kail…?' Luckley/Alnwick 1870s; **cole, keal** – potage made of colewort, Ray/North 1673; **kale** (pronounced keeal) – broth, gruel, porridge, Atkinson/Cleveland 1863; 'the kail… where mawks and caterpillars soom' Wilson/G'head 1820s. [ON kál, OE cól 'cabbage'].

Miscellaneous dishes and terms

corned beef – "my Dad would call it 'corned doggie' – mostly used for sandwiches" Merihein/Ashington.

dozzel, or **dozzle** – a paste flower on the top of a pie cover, Brockett/Nth C19/1; **pye-dozzle** – an ornament made of paste put on the lid in middle of a giblet or meat pie, *Bell MS* C19/1. [source unknown, but also used of a short cone or cylinder shape in metallurgy].

ducks – faggots (meat balls) Briscoe 2003; 'ofal concoctions… sold on 'pay night' by pork butchers, hot, with pease pudding' Blenkin/Shildon C20/2; savoury ducks, Seaham 2006; **penny duck** – this was a kind of small meatball, only made with offal and eaten with a bun, J.G., Annfield Plain, 1920s.

Durham mustard – invented by Mrs Clements in Durham in 1720 – a finely ground mustard flour from the seed that could be easily mixed to a paste.

fry – liver, Blenkin/Shildon C20/2; or a selection of meat to fry.

goggle-moggle – panackelty – a common dish on Monday, also called 'caad warmed up'. Merihein/Ashington.

haggish – two kind of, a Scottish and Northumberland dainty, both made of minced mutton, etc., the one seasoned savoury with spices and the other with currans and raisons, etc. and called a spice haggish – and boiled up in the bagg or stomach of a sheep… *Bell MS* C19/1. [source unknown].

panacalty – "a concoction of bacon, onions and sliced potatoes baked in a shallow dish in the huge oven." p.22 Hitchin/Dawdon 1910s; **panacalty** – corn beef sliced and simmered with parboiled sliced potatoes, peas, gravy and anything else you can *hoy* into it, VW re Teesside 2003; **panhagglety** New Geordie Dix; **panackalty** – a warm up of mixed food left over, Teward/Teesdale C20/mid; panhaggert, **panhagglety** – meal made from potatoes, onions and grated cheese, Briscoe 2003; **pan haggoty** – Newc. [?pan + higgelty i.e. by chance]

pan soddy – a sort of pudding made in a pan under meat, *Bell MS* C19/1.

poke-puddin' – pudding boiled in a bag, *Briscoe* 2003.

potted head – stewed meat, as sold in butchers' shops, Palgrave/Hetton 1896.

pot py – meat and dough boiled, *Dodd MS* Tanfield Lea C20/2; onion, meat and vegetables cooked in a bowl, with a sealing crust of suet mix, Blenkin/Shildon C20/2.

race-ginger – ginger (root), Dinsdale/Tees 1849. [OFr rais 'root'].

skranshum – overcooked pork skin, *Dodd MS* Tanfield Lea C20/2. [imit.].

smasher – a small standing pie of gooseberries, *Bell MS* C19/1.

tatie pod – using up left over of Sunday joint.

tatie hash – panacklety.

Beer and drink

beeswine – a fermented drink brewed at home from brown and black treacle, esp. 1920s, 1930s. Once a week, the brew was tapped for drinking, and the remained topped up with water and sugar. Ginger and/or lemon peel optional ingredients.

blaked – drunk, VW re H'pool 2003; blaked meaning inebriated: 'Ahm ganna get blaked the neyt' TH Wheatley Hill/Peterlee 2002. [from blake 'pale'?].

blashy – thin: 'poor blashy milk or beer' (Nb) Grose 1787. [imit.].

draf – brewer's grains, Bailey/Co. D'm 1810. [ME, Ice. draf 'sediment'].

drucken – drunk(en), Atkinson/Cleveland 1863. [ON drukken].

drumly – muddy, turbid: 'Aw cuddint drink't, it was sae drumly' Luckley/Alnwick 1870s. [OE dróflic 'turbid'].

flanged – drunk, S'd. 2001.

maskfat – mashing vat, for brewing, Raine/Finchale.

nappy – strong: 'this good nappy ale' *Praise of Yorkshire Ale* p.14 via *Raine MS*. [cf MDu noppigh 'shaggy, rough'].

nappy – slightly drunk: 'as soon as they grew nappy / they danc'd' glossed as 'tipsy'. p.217. C19/1. Harker/Tyne C19/1.

palatic – very drunk, S'd. Q 2001; 'politic'... with the emphasis on the second syllable' A. K. Newc 1940s. [paralytic].

pant – a public water fountain, Heslop/Tyne 1880s. [?Celtic].

sipe – to drain a pot or other vessel: 'he's siping the pots' i.e. he's draining the pots after other people's drinking, Bell MS C19/1. [OE sipian].

treacle-wow – treacle beer, Wilson/G'head 1820s.

waiter – water, Luckley/Alnwick 1870s; **watta** *Dodd MS* Tanfield Lea C20/2.

whig – soured whey with aromatic herbs in it, used by labouring people as a cooling beverage, Co. Durham 1810. [?var. of whey].

yal – ale, Bailey/Co. D'm 1810; 'tyest the **yell** and stop a bit' Wilson/G'head 1820s. [OE ealu, ON öl].

yell-house – ale-house, Robson/Tyne 1849.

Appetite and taste

aigre – sour, Brockett/Nth C19/1. [Fr].

bellywark – stomach ache, Weardale, Teesdale 2001, Heslop/Tyne 1880s, etc. [OE wærc 'pain'].

chow – to chew, to masticate, Brockett Nth C19/1. [var. of chew].

clam, clem – to starve for want of food, to be parched with thirst, Brockett Nth C19/1. [clem 'to squeeze, distress' possibly from ON].

clemmed – hungry, Atkinson/Cleveland 1863.

drouth – thirst, Atkinson/Cleveland 1863; 'wad he' slockened ony bit drouth' at he might a had', Haldane/Tyne 1890s.

drouthy – thirsty, Atkinson/Cleveland 1863. [OE drugoth].

gizen – parched: 'With parched tongues and gyzen'd throats', Wilson/G'head 1820s.

gob – the mouth, Atkinson/Cleveland 1863; 'A havent gorra asbestos gob' *VIZ* 42. [?Gael. gob 'mouth, beak'].

guise – die of thirst: 'Aa was fit to guise' Robson/Tyne 1849. [var. of guizzen].

howl-kite – a vulgar name for the belly, Brockett/Nth C19/1. [kite 'stomach'].

keck, kecken – to emit the sound consequent on choking; to decline with loathing, Atkinson/Cleveland 1863. [imit.].

kedge – to fill, stuff full, esp. [re] eating, Atkinson/Cleveland 1863; 'A's kedged' Dunn. [source unknown].

kedge-belly – a glutonous eater, Atkinson/Cleveland 1863. **kedge-belly** – a large protuberant body, a glutton, Brockett/Nth C19/1.

kite – the belly or stomach, Atkinson/Cleveland 1863. [source unknown].

painch – the stomach, Robson/Tyne 1849. [paunch].

panged – stuffed, Robson/Tyne 1849. [?poss. Link with Goth. prangan 'to stuff'].

rift – to belch; also to plow out grassland, Bailey/Co. D'm 1810. [ON rypta].

slocken – to quench, Atkinson/Cleveland 1863. [ON slokna].

smatch – a savour, flavour or taste: 'a smatch o' London', Atkinson/Cleveland 1863. [OE smeccan 'to taste of'].

squench – to quench, Dinsdale/Tees 1849. [var. of quench].

stithe – strong, stiff e.g. stithe cheese, Grose 1787. [OE stíth 'strong, harsh'].

styen-caad – stone cold, Dunn.

wairsh – insipid: 'she hezzent put ony salt i' the breid, an' its as wairsh as waiter' Luckley/Alnwick 1870s; wairsh – tasteless, Robson/Tyne 1849; **wairsh**, wairch (Tyne), wairesh (N'd), wearsh (Hex) – insipid... as food without salt, Heslop/Tyne 1880s; **walch** – insipid, waterish, Grose 1787; **walsh** – insipid, watery, Atkinson/Cleveland 1863; **welsh** or **wersh** – insipid, almost tasteless, Brockett/Nth C19/1. [?var. of wearish, wallowish].

wame – the womb or belly, *Bell MS* C19/1; **wame** (pronounced wheeam) – the belly, stomach, Atkinson/Cleveland 1863; **wyem** – the stomach: 'weary byens and empty wyem' Wilson/G'head 1820s. [var. of womb].

yare – ready: 'Ah's yare fur ma dinner', Atkinson/Cleveland 1863. [OE gearu].

Tea-time

batchler buttons – a kind of small round cake, Teward/Teesdale C20/mid.

batty – a small cake: 'Thoo shall hev a spice batty on tha borthday' Heslop/Tyne 1880s.

breed – bread, e.g. 'cheese and bread', 'butter and bread', 'jam and bread' Palgrave/Hetton 1896. [OE bréad – s.thing textured].

corran-dow – scone with currants in it, K.P., Beadnell.

dad – a blow, a thump... large slice, a lump, Brockett Nth C19/1. [imit.].

Empire biscuit – shortbread with jam and icing upon! Stockton.

gob-stick – a spoon, Brockett/Nth C19/1.

hagabag – coarse table linen, *Bell MS* C19/1. [var. of huckaback].

hell – to pour out (2nd edn) Ray/North 1673+; **heald** – to pour out: 'to heald the pot' Grose 1787; **hale** – to pour or empty out, Atkinson/Cleveland 1863; hell or hail – to pour, Bailey/Co. D'm 1810. [OE hieldan, ON hella].

knife 'n' fork tea – "stiff and blood-red" M'bro.

laced – reinforced with spirits: 'strang lyac'd tea and singin' hinnies' Wilson/G'head 1820s.

mask – to infuse, esp. tea, Atkinson/Cleveland 1863; 'mask the tea' Brockett/Nth C19/1; 'mask the tea thin am clammin', Dobson 1970s; 'wor add wife's ganna mask the tye' Heslop/Tyne 1880s. [Northern form of mash].

mast – brewed, Todd/Newc 1977 [?mashed].

niffy-naffs – small cakes, sweet tasty things to eat. Phillips/Cullercoats.

pot – an earthnware mug: 'a pot o' coffee' S'm 1990s [ME pot 'earthenware vessel'].

plush cloth – used to cover table, Crocker/Spennymoor C20/1. [Fr pluche, 'fabric with pile'].

rammy – a horn or other kind of spoon, Heslop/Tyne 1880s. [ram's horn?].

samidges – sandwiches: 'bacon samidges' *VIZ 72* (1995).

scabby nannie – current loaf, F.W., Annfield Plain.

shive – slice: 'a shive oh butter an breed' Bewick/Tyne 1790s; a large slice, Luckley/Alnwick 1870s; a slice, Ferryhill 2001. [ME sheve, ON skíva].

shive – to slice (a loaf), Dinsdale/Tees 1849.

singin hinnee – cake cooking noisily, Dodd MS Tanfield Lea C20/2; **singin'-hinny** – cake with currants and butter in it, and baked over the fire on a girdle, Wilson/G'head 1820s; **singing hinny** – a kind of girdle-cake, common among old folk. (Name imported from the North.) Now generally called Spice Cake, Palgrave/Hetton 1896; **singin-hinnie** or **stinging-hinny** – a rich kneaded cake; indispensable in a pitman's family, Brockett/Nth C19/1; **singin-hinny** – a richly kneaded currant cake, rolled out thin, and baked on a girdle. It is served up hot, sliced and buttered. It is an especial favourite in N'd, Heslop/Tyne 1880s; **singing hinny** – rich scone, large as whole griddle. G'head. [name said to come from the quantity of butter causing them to fiz on the griddle].

sly cake – two layers of pastry with currants between, Belmont 2006.

spice – gingerbread Newcastle 1830s; spice – dried fruit. Hence, spice-cake, a cake full of currants, Newcastle 1830s; spice – the only name known for currant-cake. 'Cake' always means tea-cake, Hetton-le-Hole 1896. [Fr espice].

spice cake – the basic, un-iced, rich fruit cake, Blenkin/Shildon C20/2.

steash – fruit cake, Teward/Teesdale C20/mid. [source unknown].

team, teem – to empty out, to pour off or away; to pour or rain heavily, Atkinson/Cleveland 1863; **teem** – to pour out, as from one vessel to another, Ray/North 1673; **teem** – to pour out, Oxnard/Hetton 1990s; **teem** – to pour out: 'teem oot the milk' Luckley/Alnwick 1870s; to 'teem out' is to pour out liquids. A teapot with a well-turned spout is called a 'good teemer', Palgrave/Hetton 1896. [OE teman, ON toema 'to empty out'].

teas – used in the plulal thus 'No, thank you, we've hadden our teas' (but, 'my tea'), Palgrave/Hetton 1896.

thyve cake – a cheap fruit cake to spread with butter, Teward/Teesdale C20/mid. [source unknown].

whum'le – to invert as a basin or bowl over a plate of cut bread to keep it moist. Robson N'd C19/2

wigs – teacakes. Phillips/Cullercoats.

wowy an' bread – bread and treacle, Dunn. [source unknown].

Ceremonies

bride-ale – the marriage feast at a rustic wedding, Brockett/Nth C19/1.

carlins – "choice grey-peas, of the preceding autumn, steeped in spring water for 12 to 15 hours, till they are soaked or macerated; then laid on a sieve, in the open air, that they may be externally dry. Thus swelled, and enlarged to a considerable size, and on the verge of vegetating, they are put in an iron pot, or other wise, on a slow fire, and kept stirring. They will then parch, crack and as we provincially call it, bristle: when they begin to burst, they are ready to eat." Gent. Mag 1788 re N'd; Another method adopted is to fry the carlins with fat, and season highly with pepper and salt. [As well as grey peas] "the large peas of a brownish yellow spotted colour, called 'brandlings'… are much fancied and in request for carlins" Heslop/Tyne 1880s; **carlins** – grey peas steeped in water for a time, then 'bristled' and mixed with butter and sugar; they are eaten on the Sunday before Palm Sunday, Luckley/Alnwick 1870s; **carlings** – grey peas with black spot (N'd); "carlings – very hard orangish peas/pigeon food (and good for pea-shooters)" JR Sacriston C20/2.

Carling-day or **Carling-Sunday** – The second Sunday preceding Easter, when parched peas are served up at most tables in Northumberland, Grose 1787; **Carling Sunday** – Fifth Sunday in Lent, on which day the traditional dish is one of 'carlin's' cooked in melted butter. A carling (kaa:lin) is a kind of pea, of a dark grey or brown colour. They are used by lads on 'Carlin' Sunday' for throwing at one another, and are boiled by publicans for their customers on that night, Palgrave/Hetton 1896. [ON kerling 'old woman' or Care+ling].

churn-supper, corn supper – the Northumberland festival on conclusion of harvest, *Bell MS* C19/1.

dumb-cake – a species of dreaming-bread, Brockett/Nth C19/1; a cake made in silence on St. Mark's Eve, with numerous ceremonies, by maids, to discover their future husbands, Halliwell.

egg-boolin' – egg rolling: 'egg-boolin' technology' Dobson 1970s [bowling].

jarping – to hit hard-boiled eggs together to see which one broke, HP Cockfield C20; **jawp** – to shake liquid: 'Jawp an egg' is to break it, 'Jawping eggs' a gambling game with eggs at Easter, *Bell MS* C19/1; holder of uncracked egg wins the cracked one, Blenkin/Shildon C20/2. [source unknown].

kern-baby – an image dressed up with corn at a harvest home, Brockett/Nth C19/1; kern-baby – an image, or possibly only a small sheaf of the newly-cut corn, gaily dressed up and decorated with clothes, ribbons, flowers, etc., and borne home rejoicingly [at the end of] the harvest, Atkinson/Cleveland 1863; kern-baby – an image dressed up with corn, carried before the reapers to their mell-supper or harvest-home, Grose 1787. [?corn-].

kern-supper – a supper given to the working people by the farmer on the completion of shearing or severing the corn, Atkinson/Cleveland 1863; churn or kern-supper – harvest home Brockett/Nth C19/1; kirn or kurn – the harvest home in Northumberland, at which there is generally a Supper, called the Kirn Supper, *Bell MS* C19/1.

Mell-doll – an image of corn, dressed like a doll, carried... on the last day of reaping. [same as] kern-baby, Brockett/Nth C19/1. [ON mele 'corn'].

Mell Supper – a supper and merry-making on the evening of the concluding reaping day – the feast of harvest home, Brockett/Nth C19/1; mel-supper – a supper and dance given at harvest home, Bailey/Co. D'm 1810; 'the great celebration of the Mell held at the end of leading (in of the harvest) was vanishing at the turn o the century' Hartley p.64.

the **Mother of the Meal Kist** is given in the North as [a] toast – which is a 'reeking midden', *Bell MS* C19/1.

need-fire – fire obtained by rubbing two pieces of dry wood together, Heslop/Tyne 1880s. [OE nied-fyr, Norw naudeld].

Paste or **Pace eggs** – hard-boiled eggs that were rolled down a hill at Easter time. Usually had been dyed by onion skins or decorated, HP Cockfield C20; **Pace-eggs** – eggs boiled hard and stained of divers colours [used] on Easter Monday and Tuesday as playthings for children and secondly as a viand, Atkinson/Cleveland 1863; **Pace egg** – hard-boiled coloured egg, Ferryhill 2001 [OFr Pasche from Latin].

Wake – a [commemorative] feast, Atkinson/Cleveland 1863; watching over the dead the night before the funeral.

Yule-clog – the large log specially provided for burning and burnt on Christmas Eve, Atkinson/Cleveland 1863. [OE geol, ON jól].

Yule-doo – "is a kind of currant cake made in shape of a baby and given to children at Christmas. Not so many years ago the 'putter lad' expected his 'hewer' to bring him the 'yule-doo.' If the hewer failed to bring one, the putter would take the hewer's clothes, put them into a 'tub,' fill it up with rubbish, and send it 'to bank'; or if the 'doo' was not well made, the putter nailed it to a tub and wrote the hewer's name underneath" Palgrave/Hetton 1896; a figure of a woman made of paste and spices meant as a remembrance of the Virgin Mary, given to young persons on Christmas Day, *Bell MS*, Newc 1820s; **Yule doo** – a small image made of dough, with a couple of currants for eyes, Luckley/Alnwick 1870s; **Yull-doo** – gingerbread man with hands joined, Newcastle 1970s; **yell-do** – Yule dough. A sort of cake with currants and spice. "My mother's brothers, when they were lads working at the pit used to get their Yell do's on New Years Eve from the men they putted for – usually a spicy teacake and a shilling. When I was little, Granddads used to ask if you'd getten your **Yell do** – "I just thought they meant Christmas presents. But the expression is still used today when a present of money is given – a father will give his grown up son his Yell do for a Christmas or New Year drink. I have heard my husband use it. Perhaps it is only used among pit folk" Stan Oxley/High Thornley.

Children's food

boily – staled bread soaked with hot milk and lashed with sugar. S'd; "**boilee** – that to me is a slice of white bread put in a basin, sprinkled with sugar and then some warmed milk poured over. It was spoon fed to babies as their first solids, weaning them." Merihein/Ashington.

bullets – sweets: 'bullets en spice' Armstrong/Tanfield C20/2; bullets or kets – sweets, Sterling/H'pool C20; 'black bullets en mint losengers' Egglestone/Weardale C19/2; bullet – a round sweetmeat, Heslop/Tyne 1880s; sugar bullets – sweets, James Hay WW1; Nelson's bullets – a sweetmeat in the shape of small balls, Dinsdale/Tees 1849; black bullets – black or sometimes brown spherical boiled mint sweets made by Welch's of Tyneside called Tyne Mints on the jar, Sanderson/Easington 1950s.

candy – sweets: 'candy see mickle a nounce', Egglestone/Weardale C19/2.

claggum – treacle made hard by boiling, Luckley/Alnwick 1870s; claggum – treacle lollipops, etc. Atkinson/Cleveland 1863; called in other places in the North, **clag-candy, lady's-taste, slittery, tom-trot, treacle-ball,** and **toughy**, Brockett Nth C19/1. [clag 'to stick'].

coggie – an apple core, RM Norton C20/mid.

colley – butcher's meat. A term chiefly among children, Brockett Nth C19/1. [ON kolla 'cow'].

dip – hot fat and meat juices off the Sunday joint. "Ya muther would give yi a slice of bread dipped in this to keep going till the dinner was ready" N.Wilson/Newburn.

drippin – this was the fat and meat juices when it was cold., you got this spread on bread for ya supper. N.Wilson/Newburn.

Gibraltar Rock – veined sweetmeat, sold in lumps resembling a rock, Brockett/Nth C19/1.

goodies – sugar sweetmeats for children, Atkinson/Cleveland 1863.

gowk – apple core Blenkin/Shildon C20/2, etc.; **gowker** – apple core, South Moor 2003.

goke – the central portion of anything, as the core of an apple, the yolk of an egg, Atkinson/Cleveland 1863. [OE geolca].

gowie – chewing gum, S'd 2001.

ket – sweets, especially the cheap and nasty kind: "That's not proper chocolate, that's just ket!" (Horden, Murton 1960s); cheap sweets. Phillips/Cullercoats. [?from ket – see next section]

scranchum – a sort of thin hard-baked spice or ginger bread, *Bell MS* C19/1; scranchum – gingerbread baked in thin wafers, Briscoe 2003. [imit.].

sweeties – confections or sweetmeats for children, Brockett/Nth C19/1.

taffy – toffee, candy made from a mixture of butter, or dripping and sugar, baked till quite hard. Claggum is the same, but with treacle as the ingredient instead of sugar, Heslop/Tyne 1880s.

Bad food

aig – sourness: 'the milk has got an aig' Brockett/Nth C19/1. [Fr].

bishop – to scorch or burn meat, Bell MS C19/1. ['because the bishops burn who they lust and whosoever displeaseth them' – Tindale].

deaf, defe – decayed generally: 'deaf nut', 'deaf earth'. The pronunciation is defe. [OE déaf].

fire-fanged – of food, 'burnt', of persons, fierce, Atkinson/Cleveland 1863. [fire-seized, or fire-bitten].

foist – to smell musty, Brockett Nth C19/; 'corne will foyst with lyinge long in the garner' Best's Farming Book 1641 p.103 via *Raine MS.*

foisty – musty, Dinsdale/Tees 1849; foisty – moudly, 'foisty pies', Dobson 1970s. [OFr fust 'a cask'].

fozy – soft and spongey, generally applied to frosted turnips, Luckley/Alnwick 1870s; fozy – unsound, of vegetables. A 'fozy' turnip is a woolly one, Palgrave/Hetton 1896. [cf. Du voos, Norw fos 'spongey'].

ket – filth, offal, carrion, Dinsdale/Tees 1849; ket – stinking, unhealthy, diseased: 'ket meat/deed ket' – [meat from] animals dying a natural death, Heslop/Tyne 1880s; ket – carrion; tainted meat, Atkinson/Cleveland 1863. [ON kjöt 'flesh'].

ketty – putrid, Atkinson/Cleveland 1863.

kizoned or **kizzened** – parched or dried: 'kizzened meat' – meat too much roasted, Brockett/Nth C19/1; **kizzen** – any thing in cooking which has got burnt and dried, *Bell MS* C19/1. [?var, of guizzen].

mauk, mawk – a maggot, Brockett/Nth C19/1. [ON mökr].

ram – fetid, Atkinson/Cleveland 1863; acrid or pungent (of a smell) Dinsdale/Tees 1849; rancid (re butter. bacon) Blenkin/Shildon C20/2. [cf. Ice. ramr].

rated – approaching to rottenness, Bailey/Co. D'm 1810. [source uncertain].

reesty – applied… to bacon when it is rancid, Luckley/Alnwick 1870s; reasty – rancid, particularly applied to bacon spoilt by long keeping, Brockett/Nth C19/1. [OFr resté 'left over, stale'].

Sources of glossary

Allen: D. Elliston Allen (1968) *British Tastes: an enquiry into the likes and dislikes of the regional consumer* (London).

Alnwick 1870s – John Lamb Luckley's *The Alnwick Language* (Newcastle Central Library).

Atkinson/Cleveland 1868: *A glossary of the Cleveland dialect* by J.C. Atkinson (London, 1868).

Bailey/Co. Durham 1810: *John Bailey's General view of the agriculture of the County of Durham* (1810).

Bell MS Newc 1820s: Newcastle University Bell/White MS 12.

Bewick: Thomas Bewick (1850) *The howdy and the upgetting* (London).

Briscoe 2003: Diana Briscoe *Wicked Geordie English* (London, 2003).

Brockett/Nth C19/1: John Trotter Brockett *A glossary of North Country words in use...* (Newcastle, 1825, 2nd edn 1829, 3rd edn 1846).

Crocker: Jean Crocker 'in conversation with a lady from Spennymoor concerning words which related to household objects ...used normally in her young days,' and published in *Accent on the North East: Dialect jottings* (Darlington, 1983).

Dobson 1970s: Scott Dobson (various booklets, Newcastle).

Dodd MS – Word list by Michael Dodd C20/2, in Beamish Regional Resources Centre.

Dunn: Nelson Dunn *Dinna taak si fond* (tape cassette, 2002) [re Bishop Auckland ca.1950].

Eveleigh – David J. Eveleigh (1986) *Old cooking utensils* (Aylesbury).

Harker/Tyne – *Songs from the Manuscript Collection of John Bell* ed. D. Harker (Surtees Society vol.196, 1985).

Halliwell: J.O. Halliwell (1847) *A Dictionary of Aechaic and Provincial Words* (2 vols, London).

Hartley, M. & Ingleby, J. (1972) *Life in the Moorlands of North-East Yorkshire* (London).

Heslop/Tyne (1880s): R. Oliver Heslop *Northumberland Words: A glossary of words used in the County of Northumberland and on the Tyneside* (2 vols, English Dialect Society, 1893–4).

Hetton-le-Hole 1896: F.M.T. Palgrave: *A list of words and phrases in everyday use by the natives of Hetton-le-Hole in the County of Durham* (English Dialect Society vol.74, 1896).

Hitchin (1962) George Hitchin *Pit-Yacker* (London).

Hull/wNewc 1880s: Rev. J.E. Hull *A popular intoduction to the Tyneside Dialect* (typescript in the Archives of the Natural History Society of Northumbria).

Kennet MS: Bishop Kennet's 'Etymological Collections of English Words and Provincial Expressions', British Library MS Lansdowne 1033.

Merihein/Ashington – Florie Merihein.

Moorman: F.W. Moorman (1916) *Yorkshire Dialect Poems* (London).

Newcastle 1900: D. Embleton *Local dialect dialogues* ca.1897.

Newcastle 1960s: Cecil Geeson *A Northumberland and Durham word book* (Newcastle, 1969).

Nicholson 1880: W.E. Nicholson *A glossary of terms used in the coal trade of Northumberland and Durham* (Newcastle, 1880).

Orange/Bebside – Ronald Orange re Bebside (Horton Grange Colliery).

Oxley/High Thornley – Joyce Oxley (High Thornley, now Forest Hall).

Phillips/Cullercoats – Joan Taylor Phillips Cullercoats.

Raine MS: British Library MS Egerton 2868.

Raine/Finchale: *Deeds of Finchale Priory* ed. J. Raine (Surtees Society, vol.6, 1837).

Robson N'd C19/2 – Helena H. Clark 'More Northumbrian Lore: Extracts from the diaries of a north country naturalist' *Jnl Uni of Newc Agricultural* Soc 21 (1967) 3–7 [from diaries of Charles Robson, Northumbrian layabout, 1881 moved to Birtley, Co. D'm. Died 1924 aet.78. Extracts from diaries of 1879–1899 period, presumably remarking on local (D'm) usage…]

Staithes 1930: Stanley Umpleby *The Dialect of Staithes.*

Teward/Teesdale C20/mid – Kathleen Teward *Teisdal' en how twas spok'n* (Teesdale, 2003) [re Newbiggin-in-Teesdale].

Wilson/G'head 1820s: Thomas Wilson (1826–1830) *The Pitman's Pay* (Newcastle).

N. Wilson/Newburn – Norman Wilson.

'Scotswood Road Tea Company' by Jimmy Forsythe (1958).

Tyne & Wear Archive service. P.6/39.

Part four – dialect texts

Here is a place for some of those poems and proses too long to fit into the text, but illustrating our many themes of cooking and provisions. These are arranged (loosely) in date order, so be prepared to a mix of subjects, from wild game to stocking a shop and the best way to cook bacon (or a clock!)…

1. Two Fairy Tales from 'The Denham Tracts' (reprinted Newcastle, 1975)

The Rumshaugh Kirnin'

Once upon a time a ploughman was engaged with his team, consisting of two horses, and two oxen, with a boy to guide them, in tilling a field near Rumshaugh, in the parish of Simonburn, reputed to be haunted by Fairies. When turning his cattle at one of the land's ends, he hears a great kirnin' [churning] going on somewhere near him. He made another circuit, and on listening was aware of a doleful voice lamenting, "Alack! A-day, I've broken my kirn-staff! What will I do?" "Give it me, and I'll mend it", cries the ploughman; and on his return from the next bout, he found the broken kirn-staff along with hammer and nails. He repaired and left it: and on taking another turn with his team, it was gone, and a liberal supply of bread and butter set down in its place. He and the boy partook of it, and also the cattle, except one ox, which resisted all efforts to force the food upon it. Before they got to the land's end, the stubborn brute dropped down dead – a victim to Fairy vengeance!

[p.133]

Brunt and scadded

At Rothley Mill there was a kiln for drying oatmeal, which the Fairies used to visit every night to make porridge. The miller's lad, one evening, thought he would gar them loup [make them jump]; and looking in at the top of the kiln, and seeing them sitting round their cauldron stirring the porridge, he took up a stone, and throwing it into the pot, the porridge flew about. The fairies all jumped up; and everyone of them crying – Brunt and scadded! Brunt and scadded! [burnt and scalded] ran after the lad, and overtook him just as he reach a stile between the mill and Rothley; when one of them gave him a blow on the back – and from that time he always went lame.

[pp.46–7]

2. From 'The Pitman's Wedding' (Edward Chicken, ca.1720)

This classic is an educated Newcastle schoolman satirising the manners of the mining folk of Benwell – here the marriage feast of the pitman and his lass.

Then Haste is made, the Table clad,

No Patience till the Grace is said:

Swift to the smoking Beef they fly;

Some cut their Passage thro' a Pye:

Out streams the Gravy on the Cloth;

Some burn their Tongue with scalding Broth:

But <u>rolling</u> Spices make them <u>fain</u>,

They shake their Heads, and sup again:

Cut up that Goose, cries one below;

And send us down a Leg, or so:

An honest Neighbour tries the <u>Point,</u>

Works hard, but cannot hit a Joint:

The Bride sat nigh, she rose <u>in Prim,</u>

And cut, and tore her Limb from Limb.

Now Geese, Cocks, Hens, their Fury feel,

Extended Jaws devour the Veal:

Each <u>rives</u>, and eats what he can get;

And all is Fish that comes to Net:

Notes:

Rolling – rolling about their mouths i.e. chewing, savouring?

Fain – glad

Point – i.e. is the carving knife sharp?

In prime 'to single out the prey' (a hunting term)

Rives – tears, rends

3. 'The Bonny Moor Hen' (ca.1818)

Lack of food and rights on commonland is the theme of the more radical 'The Bonny Moor Hen'. The Bishop's authority sought to stop the lead miners of Weardale shooting red grouse on those open lands he nominally controlled. In 1818 this led to a confrontation between the forces of Law and those of free-shooting. The song could have been written quite close to the event it portrays; it was certainly popular at fairs throughout the mid-nineteenth century and re-published with an informative historical introduction by Wm. Egglestone in 1874 (re-issued in turn as a pamphlet by the small press, Strong Words, from Whitley Bay, in 1979). In Egglestone's opinion, it could have been the work of a local schoolmaster, Thomas Coulson; but its apparent carelessness with the facts (the Wm Hedley hinted at in the text may not have been there at all, nor the six-footer, Thomas Elliott) query the accuracy of any local knowledge, while its popular commercial style, only slightly dialectal, suggest it is not (in its surviving form) specially folkic.

You brave lads of Weardale, I pray lend an ear,
The account of a battle you quickly shall hear
That was fought by the miners, so well you may ken,
By claiming a right to their bonny <u>moor hen</u>.   red grouse

Oh this bonny moor hen, as it plainly appears,
She belonged to their fathers some hundreds of years;
But the miners of Weardale are all valiant men,
They will fight till they die for their bonny moor hen.

These industrious miners that walk in their clogs,
They suit them to travel o'er mountains and bogs;
When the bonny moor hen she mounts up in the air,
They will bring her down neatly, I vow and declare.

Oh the miners in Weardale, they are bred to the game,
They level their <u>pieces</u> and make sure of their aim;   guns
When the shot it goes off – Oh the powder doth sing,
They are sure to take off either a leg or a wing.

Now, the times being hard and provisions being dear,
The miners were starving almost we do hear;
They had nought to depend on, so well you may ken,
But to make what they could of the bonny moor hen.

There's the fat man of <u>Oakland</u>, and Durham the same,   Auckland i.e. bishop's men
Lay claim to the moors, likewise to the game;
They sent word to the miners they'd have them to ken,
They would stop them from shooting the bonny moor hen.

Oh these words they were carried to Weardale with speed,
Which made the poor miners to hang down their heads;
But sent them an answer, they would have them to ken,
They would fight till they died for their bonny moor hen.

A captain was wanted at the head of the clan,
<u>H-Y</u>, of great Oakland was chose for their man;   ?Hedley
Oh, his legs were too small, and not fit for the stocks,
His scalp not being hard for to suffer the knocks.

Oh this captain he had a black bitch of his own,
That was taught by the master 'twas very well known;
By the help of his bitch he'd met many a one,
And when he comes to Weardale he'll do what he can.

Oh, this captain says, I am but a stranger here,
My bitch and myself is a match for a deer;
Either beggars or tinkers, she will pull off their bags,
And if that will not do she will <u>rive</u> them to rags.   tear

So this army set out from high Oakland, we hear,
H-Y in the front, and black bitch in the rear;
On they marched to Wolsingham, then made a halt
And concerning the battle began to consult.

They heard that the miners' grand army was strong,
The captain that led them was full six feet long;
That put Mr Wye in a bodily fear,
And back to great Oakland he wished for to steer.

Up spoke the game-keepers: cheer up, never fear,
Through Stanhope and Weardale our way we will clear;
In Durham or Oakland it shall never be said,
That by a few miners our army was <u>paid</u>.   beaten

So the army set off straightway, as we hear,
And the miners' grand army did quickly appear:
Oh, they fired along till their powder was done,
And then they laid on with the butt ends of their guns.

They dismounted the riders straightway on the plain,
H-Y and black bitch in the battle were slain;
Oh they that ran fastest got first out of town,
And away they went home with their tails hanging down.

Oh this battle was fought all in Stanhope town,
When the chimneys did <u>reek</u> and the soot it fell down;   smoke
Such a battle was ne'er fought in Stanhope before,
And I hope such a battle will ne'er be fought more.

Oh this bonny moor hen, she's gone o'er the plain,
When summer comes back she'll return here again;
They will <u>tip</u> her so neatly, that no one'll ken   touch
That ever they <u>rivall'd</u> the bonny moor hen.   disputed over

Oh this bonny moor hen, she has feathers <u>[e]new</u>,   enough
She has many fine colours, but none of them <u>blue</u>;   i.e. the colour of a uniform
Oh the miners of Weardale they are all valiant men,
They will fight till they die for the bonny moor hen.

4. A Feast from Thomas Wilson's 'Pitman's Pay' (1830)

Thomas Wilson, writing in the 1820s, portrays pitmen tucking into a meal in very much the way they tackled a seam of coal:

But christenin's now are <u>suiner duin</u>   sooner done
By far than what they us'd te be;
Folks were not <u>ax'd</u> for efternuin   asked
Te get blawn out wi <u>blashey</u> tea: weak

For <u>nowse</u> but solids then wad please—   nothing
Substantials that wad bide some cuttin'—
A ham and veal, a <u>round</u> and peas,   i.e. of beef?
Some <u>turmits</u> and a leg o' mutton;   turnips

A dumplin like a sma' coal heap—
A <u>puil</u> o' spice <u>kyel</u> i' the middle--   pool / broth
Wi' pies and puddins, wide and deep,
About myed up the savory <u>siddell</u>.   schedule

Here there was plenty gawin' and comin'—
Here we cou'd <u>cut</u> and come agyen—   carve (help themselves)
And a' wesh'd down, by men and women,
Wi' bumpers frae the awd <u>grey hen</u>.   stone bottle

This was the kind o' <u>belly timmir</u>   belly timber (food)
For myekin PITMEN strang and tuiff,
But now they run them up far slimmer
Wi' tea and other weshy stuff.

Splash gan the <u>spuins</u> amang the <u>kyell</u>—   spoons / broth
<u>Di'el</u> take the hindmost on they <u>drive</u>—   Devil / excavate
Through and through the bowl they <u>wyell</u>—   sift (re sorting coal)
For raisins how they stretch and strive.

This ower, wi' sharp and shinin' <u>geer</u>	tools
They now begin their <u>narrow workin'</u>,	hewing
Whilst others, eager for the beer,	
Are busy the grey hen uncorkin'.	

Tho' still they're i' the <u>hyel</u> a' hewin',	coalface
Before they close the glorious day,	
They <u>jenkin a' the pillars down</u>,	slim the support pillars
And efter tyek the <u>stooks</u> away.	last bits

5. 'The Soop Kitchin' (Ned Corvan)

(Tune – "Lilla's a Lady")

While this is a fine and amusing piece of social observation, there is something cruel in Corvan's satire (compare his slightly callous treatment of 'The Fire upon the Quay'). It is hard to deal with the topic of charity and acknowledge the persistence of need. Of the mid-twentieth century Charles Trelogan remembered:

"Near Xmas some villages provided a meal for the aged and at a bus stop I met one of the recipients to be told he had enjoyed himself: 'It was knife an' fork and ard 'ev getting 'am [ham] if ard been one seat farther on. But a gorra pickly good pie in place of, an' ars gannen back next yor.'"

The soup kitchin's open- then cheer, Christians, cheer!	
What glorious news for poor starvin' sowls here!	
The soup kitchin's open for a' sorts in need;	
So rush in wi' yor tickets- ye'll get a gud feed.	

Chorus
| O fine, het steem soop! O bliss that steem soop! | |
| Aw likes maw drop o' soop! | |

It's myed oot o' beef <u>hoffs</u>, fine barley, an' peas;	houghs, upper leg
Smokin' het, it's dilishus te sup at <u>yen's</u> ease;	one's
It's gud for the rich, an' not bad for the poor;	

Gox! empty <u>kite</u> grumlers it's sartin te cure.   stomach

Spoken – Drop that spoon, spooney! D'ye want te myek maw spoon the bone o' contenshun, eh? Bring this chep a ladle, mistres, an' a <u>basin</u>. Next the bottom, he wants sum thick. What a wite [weight] that soop's tyekin frae maw mind! Begox! it's run inte the channels o' maw corporation; an now aw feel like an alderman efter a gud feed! It's a fine institushin; it suits maw constitushin; an tiv [to] onny poor sowl in a state o' destitushin it's a charitable contribushin. Sum people's born wi' silver spoons i' thor gobs, but it strikes me mine's been a basin o' soop. They enjoy the luxeries o' this world; A-whey, nivver mind – just gi' me the sweet soond o' spoons an' basins. That's the music that bids me discorse! It fills me wi' delight! Thor's nowt can <u>lick't</u>. [beat it]

(Tune – 'Merry Haymakers')

Then a song an' a cheer for the rich spreed o' steem
O' the soop floatin' roond us on high;
For the givers an' the makers, the tickets an' the Quakers,
An' subscribers that nivver tip shy.

We blaw oot owr <u>bags</u> on the cheep ivvery day,   stomachs
While happy as kings there we <u>mess</u>;   eat a meal
Gox! us poor starved sowls nivver heed the wind that howls,
For close roond the tyebles we press.

(Tune – 'Cameron Men')

Roond tyebel and benches the <u>bullies</u> they stick,   companions, keelmen
A' cled in thor feedin' array;
Sum coolin' het soop, uthers fishin' for thick,
Uthers waitin' thor torns i' dismay.

Then we hear the spoons rattlin', rattlin', rattlin',
We hear them agyen an' agyen;
Thor knockin' thor basons an' <u>brattlin'</u>,   making a noise
'Tis the voice o' the brave Sandgit men.
Bob Johnson cries, "How! becrike, men, what's that?"
Wiv his spoon raised up high for te view;
"Begum! it's a rat, or a greet lump o' fat"-
Says Ranter, "It's mebbies sum stew!"

Then we hear the spoons rattlin'. rattlin', rattlin',
Ye hear them agyen an' agyen;
"Shuv the salt roond!" aw hear sum chaps prattlin',
'Tis the voice o' the brave Keeside men.

The Paddies flock in wi' the rest iv a trice,
Then doon to thor basins they stoop;
Says Mick, "It's cock turtle!" Says Barney, "It's nice!
Made from real Irish bulls – O what soop!"

Spoken – "Long life t' the soop kitchin!" says Mick. "An' hivven be his bed thit invented it!" says Barney. "What's this?" says Mick. "Och! it's only a bone. Be jabers! I thought it was a lump of lane bafe [lean beef]. Some moor, misthress!"

Then ye hear the spoons rattlin', rattlin', rattlin',
Once mair ye hear them agyen;
Ye hear them prattlin', prattlin', prattlin',
'Tis the voice o' the Callaghan men.

The Sandies, frae Scotland, they join i' the group,
Sweerin' oatmeal's oot-dune wi' sic stuff,
As wi' gud <u>Heelin'</u> stamocks they swalley the soup   Highland
In thor <u>wames</u>, till they scarcely can puff.   bellies

Spoken – "It's capital stuff, Sandy; and vera economical." "A capital remairk," says Watty

Then ye hear the spoons rattlin', rattlin', rattlin',
Ye hear them agyen and agyen;
Ye hear them prattlin' an' prattlin',
'Tis the voice o' the Cameron men.

6. 'Marla Hill Ducks Imprisoned For Trespassing' (Tommy Armstrong)

One of Tommy Armstrong's finest satires. The claims by land-owners over commonland, where village ducks and the like might feed freely, is given the full legal (and religious) treatment.

Noo if ye'll <u>pae</u> itenshin a moment or two,	pay
Aw'll tell ye a storee aw <u>naw</u> to be true.	know
It a small collry village tha <u>caul</u> Marla Hill,	call
For to tell the <u>suiam</u> storee thar's men liven still.	same
It's <u>abeot</u> twenty ducks thit went oot for te play	about
Upon a <u>aud pastor</u>, one fine sumor's day;	old pasture
But the farmer ispied them, en <u>teuk</u> them wholesale,	took
En <u>fund</u> them fresh lodgings in Marla Hill Jail.	found
Noo the pastor tha plaid on wis worthlis en bare.	
Thor wasint a blaid a green grass growen thair;	
<u>Tha</u> had been trespasen, en coudint deni'd,	they
But, like uthor prisnors, tha shud a been tried.	
Wivoot judge or joory, he teuk them away,	
He nivor once <u>ax't</u> if tha had owt to say;	asked
If he'd <u>geen</u> them a chance, tha wid awl geten bail,	given
But he teuk them <u>is</u> prisnors to Marla Hill Jail.	as
Noo in Marla Hill prisin tha hadint been lang,	
Till tha ax'd one anuther wat had tha <u>dun rang</u>,	done wrong
Thit tha sud be captord en closely confined	
In a dark dreery dungin be Marla Hill <u>hind</u>.	farm official
<u>Tha nue</u> vary weel thit tha <u>warnit it yem</u>,	they knew / weren't at home
En ta be see ill-treated tha thowt 'twis a <u>shem</u>;	shame
It <u>muaiks</u> me sorry to tell ye th' tale	makes
Aboot th' young prisnors in Marla Hill Jail.	

For days tha were lock'd up, <u>buaith</u> hungry en drie,   both
But to <u>brick</u> th' door opin tha thowt tha wid trie   break
<u>We</u> thor <u>nebs</u> en thor claws tha sune muaid a road throo   with/beaks
Wen th' hind wis it wark wi his horses and <u>plue</u>.   plow

Sixteen of th' twenty got nicely away,
<u>Tha</u> quack'd en tha shoot'd, is much is ta sae: they
"O liberty's sweet," en kept waggin' thor tail,
En that's hoo tha <u>gat oot</u> a Marla Hill Jail.   got out of

Thare wis still <u>fower</u> left in this miserable den,   four
Th' twenty belanged to three differint men;
So tha met en tha thowt th' best way for to <u>dae</u>   do (go about it)
'Twis for them to gan doon th' Land Steward to see.

The went, en wis welcom'd, he <u>tret</u> them so kind,   treated
He laid all th' blame on the Marla Hill hind;
Wile telling thor storee th' Steward <u>grue</u> pale,   grew
Wen tha teld him thor ducks wis in Marla Hill Jail.

Wen <u>leeven</u>, the Steward to them he did say: leaving
"Tell th' hind th' ducks must be awl <u>set away</u>."   freed
Tha thowt 'twis awl reet wen th' Steward tha <u>seed</u>,   saw
But th' next news th' had ta pay ninepence <u>a-heed</u>.   a head

Thar'll be ducks on th' pastor wen th' Steward en Hind
Is laid doon belaw, tike the rest of mankind:
Tha'll be sent tiv a place fer ta weep en ta wail,
Buaith th' guvnor en turn-kee of Marla Hill Jail.

7. 'Cum te maw Shop' (A Recitation for Grocers and Provision Dealers) (Joe Wilson)

At morn, when <u>frae</u> yor bed ye rise,   from
Ye shrug yor shoolders, rub yor eyes;
What d'ye want te calm, refresh? —
Wi' soap a gud an' hearty wesh;
Then ready for yor mornin's feast,
A cup o' coffee warms the breest:
For soap an' coffee aw excel—
Aw'm startin business for me-sel.

At noon, when frae yor daily toil
Yor freed te dine—the pot i' boil
Wi' broth, at <u>hyem</u>, yor heart 'ill cheer,   home
Gud dinners myek the hoose mair *dear*,
But broth, withoot thor's plenty peas
An' barley i' them, seldum please;
For barley, peas,—green, whole, an' splet,—
Cum te maw shop, the best ye'll get.

Then Time flees on wi' 'lectric wings
Till tea-time, hoosehold cumfort brings;
Each happy groop sits doon te tea,
A plissent, hyemly seet te see;
But plissent chat seun turns abuse
Withoot thor's sugar in the hoose;
For sugar—lump an' soft, wi' tea,
Thor's nyen keeps half as gud as me.   none

Then supper-time cums roond at last,
Aw wish 'twes here—aw cannet fast;
Wi' tea or coffee, <u>nowt</u> can beat   nothing
A slice o' bacon, gud an' sweet;
A piece o' cheese might de as weel,
Content wi' either ye wad feel;

Just try maw shop, it's sure te please,
Maw bacon's what ye call the cheese.

What is't ye <u>aw</u> se often need?   all
What is't that myeks the best o' breed?
The Staff o' Life, ye'll guess, aw's sure,
Wad nivvor been withoot gud <u>floor</u>;   flour
But breed, like ivry other thing,
Needs *butter*, so its praise aw'll sing:
For floor an' butter—salt an' sweet,
Aw sell the best iv ony street.

Then Sunday cums—wi' frinds te tea,
When spice-kyeks florish, weel-te-de;
When <u>corns</u> an' raisins, floor an' lard,   seeds?
Share i' the hoosewife's kind regard;
The finest raisins, lard, an' corns,
An' a', the weel-fill'd hoose adorns;
Aw nivvor brag—but gud an' cheap,
The *varry best* on <u>orth</u> aw keep.   earth

8. From 'Geordie's Last' (Harry Haldane, 1879)

Geordie and the Clock

…aa wis sayin' Aa went yen [one] day to Geordy's. He wis varry thrang [busy] wi' summic when Aa went in; but he leuk'd up wiv a 'What cheer, hinny!' An Aa sits doon quiet-like te watch him; an' away he gans te the fire an' lifts off the yetlin' [pan] boilin' an' steamin'. So, ses Aa, 'He' ye torned ceuk [cook], Geordy lad?' 'Aye,' ses he, 'she's aboot aneuf noo Aa think.' So he blaas the steam off a bit, an' heuked oot,--what d'ye think noo? Wey his aad [old] brass clock! Aa lueks forst at the clock an' then Aa leuks at Geordy. Man Aa felt queer like! Thinks Aa, sewerly Geordy canna be wrang iv his heed? But he leuks up when he'd upended the clock, an' ses he, 'Wor aad clock hes to be cleaned noos an' thens. She gets chocked up wi' dort an' grease, an' ye knaa thors nowt better nor het [hot] watter, wiv a bit o' sodda in't for meltin' an' cleanin' grease…'

Geordie and Rhubarb

Yen neet [one night] (it's eers [years] ago noo, as Aa sed afore), he gat a bit waak tiv hissel, an' dandered alang till he cam te Shields market plyece. An' as he wis stannan listenin' tiv a quack doctor wiv a reed [red] cap on, an' a lang tassel that wabbled aboot as he jaad [jawed] an' taaked aboot his 'real Turkey rhubarb,' somebody dunched [jogged] his airm an' tackled Geordy. It wis Jimmy Leetfoot, an', ses Jimmy, 'Thoo seems highly amused, Geordy; Aa could see biv the smile thoo had on 'at thoo wis takein't all in aboot the rhurbarb.' 'Aye,' ses Geordy, comin oot o' the crood, 'The beggar's sayin' 'at its real Torkey rhubarb, an' that he hes a brother in Jameeky 'at sends it ower till him twise a 'eer. The blackgaird, Aa believe, thinks 'at wor [we're] daft eneuf not te knaa [know] 'at Jameeky's iv America. He mebby thinks wor se ignorant o' g[e]ography as te take't for a toon i' Torkey. He's rubbin't up wiv a nutmeg grater, an' sellin bits on't for a penny to cure heed wark [headache], teuth wark, belly wark, esthma, broonkitis, an' dear knaas what else. An' its nowt but aad rhubarb ruts [roots] 'at he's mevvy [maybe] stowlen oot o' somebody's garden!'

9. 'Jackie Robison's Sunday Dinner' (from 'The Adventures of Jackie Robison', with variants from Catcheside-Warrington's edition)

Wor foaks aall went away to me Uncle Billy's for a halliday a while back, an' left us to leuk eftor the hoose. Thro' the week Aa managed me meals aall reet, but Aa didn't fancy bein' deun [done] oot o' me Sunday's dinnor, se Aa myed [made] up me mind to cook it mesel. Wor Polly's larnin' cookin' at some skyull or uthor, an' Aa got haad o' one o' the byuks she's bowt that tells ye hoo to de'd [do it]. Aa think it's caalled 'Beat-em', for thor's ne doot it fair whacked me.

Noo Aa let Tommy Daason inte the secret at the club on the Settorday neet, an' axed [asked] him to come in on the Sunday mornin' to help us, an' stop tiv he's [to his] dinnor as weel. Se we gat in the bits o' thing, we wanted for the job. We went to the butchor's forst, an' as Aa've elwis unnerstood that the meat nighest the bone was the sweetest, Aa axed him for a bit wiv a knockle on't. Wey, we got it, fower pund on't, but Aa cuddn't help thinkin' thor wes an aaful lot o' knockle an' vary little meat. Then we bowt a styen o' tetties [stone of potatoes], a couple o' cabbages, an' some apples for a puddin'. Aa'm aaful fond o' apple puddin'.

Weel, on the Sunday mornin', Tommy Daason torns up, and eftor we'd had a bit leuk at the hens an' the checkors, we set aboot the dinner twelve o'clock. Aa'd gotten up a fire to roast an ox, to meyk sure o' the oven. We put the meat in forst, ye knaa; but we had an aaful job becaase we cuddent find a tin big eneuf to haad it, so we ha[d] to let the shank end hang ower the edge, an' even then it tyuk us call wor time to shut the oven door.

Noo, the byuk [book] tellt us on ne accoont to forget to baste [?hit] the meat ivvory noo-an'-then, se Aa gov Tommy a bit o' the broom shank an' tellt him to lay on ivvory five minutes. Man! he myed an aaful mess aall ower the harth. Aa nivoor see'd me muthor dee'd [do it], but Polly's syentiffick cookery byuk mun be reet [must be right]. Meantimes, Aa's busy myekkin' Yorkshor puddin'. (By gum! Aa's awful fond o' Yorkshor puddin'.) The byuk said, "A pint an' a haalf o' milk, haalf a dozen big teybblespeuns o' flooer, three eggs an' a teybblespeun o' saalt." It wes a job getten them eggs emp[t]ied. The forst yen [first one] went off wiv a bang aall ower the plyece, and till we got it ootside, we thowt the drains had gyen wrang. Tommy's studdyin' chemistry at the neetskeul [nightschool] an' he said it wes like "H.2.S." Aa divvent knaa [don't know] what that means unless it's " horrible smell twice!" The second one got spilt on the tyebble [table] somehoo or uthor, but Aa knocked a bit hole in the ends o' the tuthors and sheuk them oot. They didn't want onny beatin' eftor that. Man! it wes clarty wark [messy work]!

Then Aa gets the big wooden spyun [spoon] for the flooer and saalt (the byuk said big spyuns, yo knaa), an' wez gan [was going] to mix't aall in me muthor's big pot pie basin, but Aa syun fund oot it wez over smaall, an' as Aa cuddent find nowt else, Aa mixed it aall in the pan we boil the tetties in. Be this time, thor wes an aaful smell o' bornin', an' Aa had a leuk [look] roond for'd. Tommy had started peelin' the tetties and forgot the meat, so Aa oppens the oven door an' gov it another floggin'. Then Aa had to de [do] a bit amb'lance work 'caase Tommy was fyul eneuf to cut a lump off hes thumb wi' the tettyknife.

Aa gat the Yorkshor puddin' mixed be one o'clock, but Aa could on'y get haaf on't inti the tin, but Aa telt Tommy it wad de for the morra. Aa wes beginnin' to hev me doots aboot the time we wor gaan [going] to hev wor dinners, becaase the byuk said the Yorkshor puddin' tyuk an 'oor an' a haalf an' that myed wor dinner time half past two, we elwis hev wors [ours] at one, ye knaa!

Aa tackled the tetties next, but Aa cuddent get them inti the biggest pan we hev; an' Aa knaa me muthor elwis gets a styen, 'caase Aa've oftens carried them hyem [home] of a Setterday neet. The byuk said, "put in some saalt," so Aa tellt Tommy thor wes a haalf pund packet i' the cupboard, an' he put it in. Aa cuddent find the page aboot cabbages, se we just rammed them byeth i' one pan, but it was a tight squeeze gettin' the lid on. Be this time time we wor byeth [both] boilin', an' thor wes still the apple-puddin' to myek. We kept shovellin' on the coals an' myed worsels [made ourselves] a good oven, but it got that aaful het [hot] we had to tyek wor weskits off.

Thor wes seun [soon] a varry funny smell i' the kitchen, an' Aa tellt Tommy Aa thowt the meat wes deein ower quick, an' in he gans [goes] an' gives it another good hidin'. Man! be this time Aa wes gettin' kind o' sorry for'd. Still thor wes a funny smell, an' Aa had anuthor hunt roond. Aa diddent like the way them cabbages wor deein [doing]. Aaful strang they wor! But that wasn't the smell. It wes mair like weshin day. An' begox! Aa wesn't far wrang. Tommy had putten a packet o' weshin pooder among the tetties i'steed o' saalt, an' they wor aall iv a lather. We nearlees had words ower that, an' the tetties had to gan oot to the hens.

As ivvorything wes gannin' on aall reet, Aa myeks a start on the puddin'. Aa gets the apples cut inti slices, an' two o' me fingers as weel: mare [more] amb'lance work! But thor was trouble wi' the paste, an' Aa'd forgot to buy some suet! That wes where the lard com in useful. It's a grand thing is lard. Eftor aall, the pot pie basin com in handy for the puddin', an' as Aa cuddent find ne clout [pudding-cloth] Aa tied hor up in me new reed [red] pocket-hankie an' put hor in the pan. The beuk said, "Boil aboot two oors." It wes haaf-past one then, an' that meant haafpast three for dinnor, an' Aa wes gettin aaful hungry: an' bastin' meat's a het job; so we had a go at some breed an' cheese to gan on wi', an' had anuthor leuk at the hens.

When we com back it teuk [took] us aal wor time to see yen anothers [one another] in the kitchen, an' the stythe [atmosphere] wes aaful. Tommy oppened the winda whiles Aa oppened the oven to leuk for the meat. It wes bornt tiv a cinder, and the inside o' the oven wes reed het! Aa leuked at Tommy an' Tommy leuked at me. We wor hungry afore; we wor starvin' noo. Then Aa spotted the Yorkshor puddin'. Man! it had getten up like a balloon; warse, in fact. Aa progged [prodded] it wi' one o' Polly's hat-pins, but it waddn't com doon.

So Aa flattened it oot wi' the wooden spyun, an' to myek sure We didn't get bornt puddin' as weel as bornt meat, I kept the oven door open an' stud ower it till it wes deun. It wes the funniest leukin' Yorkshor Aa've ivvor seen, but as it had to be wor forst corse noo, Aa thowt Aa wad sarve it iv a new style, so Aa teuk the lid off me tea-can an' cut it up in rings like gordle kyeks [girdle cakes]. Tommy an' me ate the bits reet away, but to think thor wes ne meat myed us feel varry bad – an' hungry. Aall iv a suddint, we wor startled wiv an aaful crackin', an' then we foond wor cup o' sorra had run ower the brim, for the bottoms o' the two pans on the fire had bornt reet oot – we had forgot to put the watter in.

We gov in then, an' Tommy an' me had wor Sunday dinnors off breed an' cheese an' Yorkshor, an' if ivvor Aa's in left at hyem agyen Aa's gan to ax mesel oot [ask myself out] to dinnor.

10. 'Hedgehog Pie' (Tommy Armstrong)

This is part of a tradition of 'food jokes' that appealed to nineteenth century miners, in punishment of food theft...

Aw'll sing ye e sang if yil paishantly wate, Aboot e grand supper thare's been it Street Gate; To eat this grand supper thare only wis two, But thae eat e <u>yell</u> hedgehog, sum <u>baiken en coo</u>.	whole / bacon and mutton
There's e chep i' th' neiborood hes a smaul dog, One day wen oot wauken, it catcht e hedgehog, So to hev e bit fun we th' prize thit he got, He thowt tive hees sel he wad <u>tuaikt</u> doon to Stott.	take it

Wen he teukt doon to Stott thae erainged wat to <u>dee</u>,   do
We Kingey en Barbor thae alwis muaid free;
Ivory time thit thae went thae wor hungry en drie,
So just fer e lark thae wad muaik them e pie.

Noo it ad to be kild befor starten to <u>skind</u>,   skin it
So thae took up e <u>mell</u> for to nock oot its wind;   mallet
Them thit wis prisint thae roard en thae <u>left</u>,   laughed
Th' chep mist th' hedgehog en broake th' mell shaft.

Th' mell wis nee use, so thae teuk e sharp nife,
Detarmind to tuaik ewae <u>progily's</u> life;   the prickly one
Thae tried for to kill him two difforent ways,
So thae ad him to droond for to finish his days.

Th' landlady's sister mauid up e pie crust
We th' best e beef fat en sum dumplin dust;
She nickt it aul roond, mauid it tender en thin,
Th' yuven wis het, en she put th' pie in.

Wen th' pie wis in keuken, thare wis en <u>aud</u> man,   and
Aw'll not tell hees nuaim – ye may <u>guest</u> if ye can;   guess it
Th' smell e' the pie muaid him smack hees aud lip;
He sais: "If aw'd e crust aw wid try for e dip."

Barbor en Kingey sat winken thor eye,
En wishen thae cud get a bit pie;
Thae wor watchin th' mistress esteed e' thor <u>gill</u>,   half of ale
Th' smell wis that nice thae cud ardly keep still.

Tom th' butcher, to sute them seun fund oot e plan,
He sais: "Drink off yor gills, be is sharp is ye can;
Gan inte th' meat hoose en lae aul things bie,
En aw'll watch th' mistris en steal ye the pie."

In th' meat house thae only had been e short while,
Wen thae saw th' pie cumen thae started to smile;
Tom sais: "Get it eaten, twis <u>fettild</u> for Stott,   made ready
If he cums he'll gan mad," Kingey sais: "Man it's hot."

For awl it wis het, thae put up wiv its sting,
"Aw <u>dee</u> like e rabbit," sais Barbor to King.   do
Thae each had e lump e hedgehog i' thor hand,
Sais Kingey to Barbor: "By jove! but its grand."

Time thae wor on eaten, thare went in e dog,
King tos't it <u>e buain</u> thit belanged th' hedgehog.   a bone
Saien, "Thare's e bit rabbit" but th' dog wadint hed.
Saes Kingey: "Thoo's <u>pawky</u>; thoo's ower weel fed."   chosey

Te get th' pie eaten, thae buaith wired in,
Te th' gravy ran off buaith thor noses en chin;
Wen Stott shoad th' skin e th' pie thit thae'd had,
Thae luckt it each uthor, en tornd vary <u>bad</u>.   ill

Sais Barbor to Kingey, "Jack aw wadin't cair,
But <u>progils</u> cums noo ware thor yused to be hair   prickles
Aw bowt e 'ard hat en aw tied it tite doon,
But th' progils cum faster, en went throo th' croon."

A raisor's nee yuse – thae buaith shave wiv e saw
Like <u>ice shogils</u> faulen, thae drop freh thor jaw;   icicles
Barbor's en trubil, Kingey far warse
He cannot lie soon or sit doon on hees a--e.

11. 'Poaching' (James Hay)

From a set of stories of James Hay (1890–1969) of Ushaw Moor, written down by his grandson Les Morgan.

Mind there wes some poachin went on in them days. Paxton, the agent, had a bit o' land round the back o' the bleezer, an it wes teemin wi hares an rabbits an aall sorts. A lot o' the lads use ta gan up wi nets an traps, but Paxton wes greedy. He aalways sent for Tegger Wilson, the pollis [policeman], an shopped them when he could.

Mind, Tegger use ta catch them. There wes nowt he liked better than a bit o rabbit pie, an many a time he just use ta tak what the'd caught, tell them ter bugger off, an say nowt. He wasn't bad durin the strike. There wes one night he caught Paddy McElevy an Joe Rostron reed-handed wi some rabbits.

"What yer got there, then?" says Tegger.

"Rabbits," says Joe.

"Aw aye?" says Tegger. "An where'd ye get them?"

"Yer knaa bloody weel where we got them!" says Paddy. "Off Paxton's land."

So Tegger just stands there. By lad, he wes a big feller, weel owwer six foot an about sivventeen stone. Built like a house end.

"Now lads, this is a warnin. Aa'll hev ter tak yers in if Aa catch yers agyen. How many kids yer got?"

"Fower," says Paddy.

"Five," says Joe.

"Aye, aall reet then," says Tegger. "Now remember what Aa've said. Gerraway yem [home], an remember, if Aa catch yers agyen Aa'll hev ter tak yers in. An by the way, Aa'll be up this stretch o road at deed on six ivvery night, so keep an eye out for us."

An then he just laughed an went away. Nivver even tyeuk [took] a rabbit off them. Aye, he wasn't bad at times, Tegger.

12. 'Me Gran'father's Breakfast' (attributed to Lisle Willis)

Old John, they called me gran 'father, an' he was a man that liked his own way.

He took good care he got it an' all…! Everythin' had to be done just as he said, both at the pit an' in the house. If it was done his way, it would be all right; but, if it wasn't, then ye could look out for trouble!

An', if there was one thing he was more particular about than anythin' else, it was his breakfast…

He'd leave the house every mornin' at ten past six. It wasn't far to the pit. Just across the way, 'cause his was the engine-wright's house at the end of the row, an' there was a special door for him into the pit-yard. An', once inside that, it wasn' t long before everybody knew that Old John was there…!

A big, imposin' figure, with a deep, forceful voice, an' a lot of frosty-whiteness about him. He always wore a stiff white collar, ye see, an' his hair was white an' all, with side-whiskers like mutton-chops, an' a beard like lather round his chin.

He was there on the job early, ready to say what had to be done that day; so everybody else had to be there early an' all, ready to do it!

Aye, me gran'father would spend a couple of hours gettin' things movin', givin' out his orders that had to be obeyed. Then, at ten past eight on the dot, he'd be back home for his breakfast. An' it had to be ready for him…!

Bacon an' eggs was what he had every mornin', so ye might think it would have been easy for me gran'mother gettin' them ready…? But, no, it wasn't just a case of poppin' them into the fryin' pan. To Old John's way of thinkin', that didn't bring out their full flavour, – what he said they had to be cooked in was a Dutch Oven.

Some of ye might remember them…? Made of iron, ye could clip them in front of the fire, an' with hooks to hang the slices of bacon on. The back had a handle on it, an' it swung over like, so ye could turn the whole thing round an' the other side of the bacon cooked. Then, at the bottom, there was a kind of trough. All the fat used to drip down into that so ye could use it for cookin' the eggs in.

Mind, it was a much slower way of cookin', an' it needed more watchin' than just ordinary fryin'. But that didn't matter…! Me gran'father knew it was the only way to cook bacon an' eggs. "Results prove it," he used to say. "They taste as different again cooked in a Dutch Oven. Ye can tell it a mile off!"

So it was no good me gran'mother complainin' that she hadn't time for clartin' on [mucking about] like that; that she had a big house to look after an' plenty of other work to do. Old John wouldn't have listened; or, if he had, he would have pointed out of the window to the pit. That was a much more complicated thing than a house; an', if he could keep his job runnin' smoothly, me gran'mother should do the same with hers… includin' usin' a Dutch Oven!

I wouldn't like ye to think, though, that she always did just as Old John said. After all, she was a woman…!

An' there were some mornin's when she'd start the housework, an' them two hours would fly past. Not until she looked at the clock, an' saw how late it was, did she realise the trouble she was in for. Either way an' all...! If she didn't use the Dutch Oven, me gran'father would be annoyed; but, if she did use it, it would mean breakfast wouldn't be ready for him at ten past eight. An' me gran'father would still be annoyed!

So what did she do...?

Why, she'd pop the bacon an' eggs into the fryin' pan an' start cookin' them. But she'd still get the Dutch Oven out. Then she'd watch from the scullery window for the first signs that Old John was makin' his way back across the pit-yard.

As soon as she saw him, me gran'mother had to act fast. Out of the fryin' pan would come the cooked bacon, an' onto the hooks of the Dutch Oven. The eggs'd follow, an' by the time Old John came into the house, sniffin' the air, there'd be nothin' to show how me gran'mother had really cooked his breakfast!

An', d'ye know, me gran'father never once found her out...!

13. 'Home is where the Hearth is' – reminiscences by Harry Peart

These are a few recollections of the role the open fire played in the lives of my family in the mining village of Cockfield in South West Durham.

The house was a typical stone built two up two down, terraced dwelling alongside the village green with an 'ever open door' propped open from around 4 am until bedtime around 9 pm.

The only water tap was just inside the front door where we drew all the water for our needs, from cooking, washing and even bathing.

One wall of the front room was dominated by a large cast iron kitchen range with a central open fire. There was a 'mantel shelf' or 'mantel piece' above the range where candle sticks, the tea caddy, a container with 'spills' for lighting pipes etc and a 'string tin' with lots of odds and ends of string for general use were stored. A couple of pieces of 'fretwork' were also sitting on the shelf, one was a pipe rack.

On one side of the fire was a 'hot air oven' and on the other side was a small cast iron tank or boiler for hot water also heated from the fire.

The fire itself was a space made from 'fire brick' at the side and back and a cast iron basket (fire bars) at the front and base that made a container to hold the fire and allow air to pass through to give a forced draught that kept the fire burning. This forced draught was often enhanced by a sheet of tin with a handle in the centre called a 'bleezer' being propped up to restrict air entry up the chimney and force the air to come through the fire from underneath the burning coal. This 'bleezer' made the fire burn fiercely with a roar as the up draught went up the chimney. A frequent alternative to the 'bleezer' a small fire shovel was propped up against the fire bars and the top of the range and a sheet of newspaper was held up against the shovel to create the forced draught. The paper rapidly began to singe and often burst into flames, hurriedly being pushed into the fire.

At the back of the fire was a large space, 'the chimney back', where we threw a couple of buckets of coal, and by using a 'coal rake' to rake coals down onto the fire as needed; it saved trips out across the backyard to the coalhouse on winter nights. Occasionally, this extra coal at the back caught fire and we then had a colossal fire raging that would 'roast an ox'. Sometimes this led to the soot that lined the chimney also catching fire and flames and smoke would be roaring out of the chimney pots on the roof. This was a common occurrence in the village, and was a source of amusement or embarrassment to villagers. The fire usually burnt itself out, but sometimes rather dramatic shovels-full of burning coals were rushed out of the house and water poured on them. Some people risked throwing water on the fire with the explosive results of shooting soot and smoke everywhere into the room. There was very rarely a need for the fire engines to be called out, for the nearest Fire station would be at Bishop Auckland about 10 miles away and by the time they arrived there would probably be a major house fire to deal with. The chimney was swept regularly by the village chimney sweep, a happening which is a tale to tell on its own.

On one side of the fire was the oven, heated from the fire via a hole at the back guarded by a square sheet of steel, with a hole drilled in it so that a poker could be inserted into it and the 'dog', as this steel was called, could be adjusted to make the hole narrower or wider to adjust the flow of air under the oven. This was one way in which my mother regulated the heat of the oven for all the various jobs form baking biscuits, cakes, bread or roasting, stewing meats, etc. The main way of regulating the optimum temperature for cooking was to prepare the fire in advance. The right amount and type of coal would be used and the poker and the bleezer used to get the fire burning as Mum wanted it. No thermometers or regulos. The oven had a door with an elaborate design of steel hinges and a heavy latched, lever knob to open and close the door tightly. Inside were adjustable steel shelves moved higher or lower depending on what was being cooked. The inside was gleaming white, from the regular 'whitewashing' that Mum did. The whole range was polished regularly with 'black lead', a liquid polish that was wiped on then buffed up with the 'black lead brush' until it gleamed.

Incidentally, the steel oven shelves also doubled as 'bed warmers' in the winter. Mum would wrap a piece of old flannelette sheet around a sheet and put it into the bed prior to us going upstairs. It was great to climb in bed and put your feet on this warm sheet before Mum came and removed it.

A heavy steel shelf protruded from just below the door, so that things could be lifted out for stirring or inspection. Above the door were two knobs attached to rods that went inside the range to control the amount of air that circulated. Below the oven, was a large cavity behind a cast iron panel where the hot air from the fire circulated under and around the oven. This cavity needed to be kept as clear as possible from soot and burnt-on materials so it was necessary at intervals to try to clean out this space. All kinds of long wire brushes were sold by the travelling 'paraffin oil' man for this job, but my mother had a unique and frightening way to clean this space out once a month. Dad was a miner and always carried a shaped, tin container on his belt to carry dynamite when he was down the pit. He often brought small pieces of dynamite home in this tin. Early in the morning Mum would rake out the ashes and cleared under the fire ready. She would crumble up a small quantity of dynamite and put it into a piece of newspaper then screw it up into a ball, like some hand made firework. She pushed this ball under the oven cavity, picked up the bleezer in one hand, like a Viking shield, and lit a long taper in the other hand. She lit the screwed up paper, and held the bleezer up against the fire opening. "BOOM" – the gunpowder exploded and out came all the soot and debris leaving the cavity clear for the easy flow of flames and hot air. As a child I was fascinated by this event, scared, yet always ready to witness it. Even as a teenager I never failed to be surprised by this piece of Domestic Pyrotechnics.

The oven was in use daily, a large session of baking was done twice a week with a separate day for bread. When I got up in the mornings to go to work at 7 a.m., the baking was finished, loaves of bread were cooling on the bottom of upturned loaf tins. Pies were sitting on wire trays, and the smell of fresh cooking was everywhere in the house. My mother made fadge loaves, teacakes, scones, cakes and lots of biscuits. Cakes with names like courting cake, twenty-minute cake, coconut pyramids, butterflies, etc., and biscuits such as custard creams, ginger parkin.

Another image that is strong for me is the making of the bread dough. This great lump of dough was pounded, thumped, squeezed, rolled on a large wooden board before being finished off in a large round tin dish like an earthenware crock, but made by a tinsmith.

This dish full of dough was covered with a clean tea towel and placed on the fender in front of the fire to rise. I recall the hessian bag of yeast; when this was empty it was washed and kept, for it could be sewn inside my father's pit jacket as a pocket (poacher's pocket) to bring home log-ends (the ends of pit props) for chopping into sticks to light the fire.

The fire itself had an extended 'trivet' that stuck out in front of the fire, and the large kettle was always there simmering, ready to make tea for any visitors. Over the fire was another hinged 'trivet' that could be dropped down for pans, kettles, etc., and there always seemed to be something heating or cooking on the cast iron grid.

My father was a miner and came home dirty after every shift. And about 10 minutes before he arrived home, a sheet of hessian was put down on the floor in front of the fire, and the galvanised 'bath tin' was brought in from the yard and filled with hot water from the boiler and pans on the fire. This brings to mind Friday nights: 'Bath Nights'. Again there is another story to tell about that event.

To complete my home on the range story, I need to move to the other side of the fire where we had this cast iron square pot (the boiler). The water was heated from the hot air and flames circulating around this tank; it sometimes would boil and bubble if the fire was too high. This was our only hot water supply other than boiled kettles or pans. We took out the water with a 'laden tin': this was a tin cylindrical container with a handle, which we very carefully immersed in the hot water to take out a can-full. You had to be very gentle and not touch the sides of the boiler with the laden tin, or you would knock off lots of rust and the water would be brown and rusty looking. If the fire was too high and the water was agitated and boiling, then the water was very brown and not very clean. There was one golden rule: if you removed hot water then you replaced it immediately with the same amount of cold water from the tap.

To close these reminiscences, I only need to close my eyes and can see the kitchen range, with the blazing fire, I can hear the crackles and bangs of the stone in the coal, I can see the imaginary pictures in the flames and I can feel the burning heat on my bare legs as I perched on one of the end boxes that were part of the fender we had. I can also feel the cold on my back from the rest of the room. I can smell the baking and cooking.

We spent long hours sitting around the fire, singing songs, or listening to the round 'Echo' radio for the obligatory news and *Children's Hour*, also *Dick Barton, Special Agent, In Town Tonight, Sing Something Simple, Music Hall*, etc.

Wall to wall carpets, central heating and digital t.v. can never replace those lost days.

I can now look back and imagine myself being 'The Fire'. What tales I could tell, as I looked out into the room where family life went on day after day. The fire was the centre of all our life events and requires a special consideration in local mining history and the very personal lives in my family.

14. 'Jasper the Chicken' by Tom Moreland

One other thing the Tagger men traded for old clothes, were 1-day-old chickens. We must have had a dozen golf ball sized, fluffy yellow chicks, running in the back garden.

It was a sight to behold. Mother threatening the Tagger man with physical violence if he did not give back father's new woollen jumper. The garment in question, and the centre of the argument, had been swapped for two chicks. In my opinion it had been a very good deal. I failed to see any problem.

Like the fish, all the chickens died, with the exception of Jasper. He defied all the odds by growing up fine and healthy, albeit with the small problem of being neurotic and utterly insane.

Jasper was vicious to the extreme. No dogs or cats entered our garden, or even walked past the front garden gate.

In the early days Jasper would sit by the gate, if any animal came past the opening he would jump on their back. Scratching at them with his claws, and then pecking at their eyes, they would flee in terror. Peace loving creatures soon learned to pass on the other side of the street.

I can still visualise Jasper sitting on the spade, while father dug the garden. Jasper would be waiting for any (soon to be eaten) earthworms that would appear on the surface, during the excavation works.

Mother ended Jasper's freedom of movement after he had chased her up the garden path. Mother was screaming like a gibbering idiot as she ran. The clothes pegs flew one way, and the clean washing ended up on the garden. The situation may not have been taken so seriously, if it had not been for us children. Sitting looking out of the dining-room window, we thought it had been a hilarious and uplifting scene.

Father's unwise answer to the situation, was to confine Jasper to the greenhouse. This crazy cockerel, unhappy at his close confinement, promptly destroyed all the tomato plants. Father was not very happy, but mother felt safe.

The only safe method of feeding, and watering Jasper, was by way of a missing window in the roof of his 'glass house'…

Come Christmas time, it was decided to invite Jasper to join us for dinner (he was to be the guest of honour).

A neighbour's son, Ronny Priest, was the only person brave enough (or daft enough) to face Jasper head on. Father gave him a couple of shillings, and elected his help in preparing Jasper for the festivities…

It was Christmas day dinnertime, and Jasper was placed in that most important of places. He was in the centre of the table with his feet in the air, and his arms tucked under his back.

At the beginning of a meal, father often teased us children. He would tell us that a lovely little bunny rabbit had been happily hopping around in a field the previous day. That same little rabbit was now lying in the tureen, in the middle of the table and under the pie crust.

'Who wants the first piece?'

That the poor innocent lamb we were about to enjoy eating had been snatched from its sad mother's side.

'Who wants the first slice?'

On this occasion there was no need to say anything. We were already in tears. Poor Jasper!

Adopting his most serious look, father put the carving knife to Jasper's chest. Try as he may, father could not slice into Jasper. To our delight, mother gave our plump, but unwanted dinner guest, to the neighbours.

We had a most welcome vegetarian Christmas dinner.

My eldest brother George would like it mentioned at this point that, not only did Ronnie Priest get paid for murdering Jasper but he also got to eat him.

15. Extracts from 'Dorfy' – 'Aal Tegither Agyen' (ca.1956) and 'Mair Geordie Taalks' (1964) – originally appearing as columns in the South Shields Gazette.

Shoppin'

Thor's one job a wife diz that sh' nivvor gets onny praise for, an' that's Shoppin'. Sh' kin trail aroond gettin' the meatiest mince at one butcher's an' the leanest chops at another's. But the fambly nivvor notices owt about them – unless tho're not prop'ly cyukked.

That the' waar specially chosen nivvor seem t' strike them, an' neebody ivvor seems t' reelise thor's mair in Shoppin' than jist gaan inte the forst grosser's y' come to an' axin' for a pund o' bacon.

In fact, in maist hyems, a wife jist gets snorted at for gaan shoppin' when sh' cud get ivrythink delivered. Last week f'rinstance, Aa wawked oot that Aa had humped fifty-fower pund o' grub hyem for me fambly – a bit at a time. But did Aa get onny gratichude for it? Not a bit. "Bigger fyul ye!" says Elee. "Ivrythink wud come up on the wagon if y' had the sense t' write yor list out at the week-end.

But onny housewife knaas watt writin' a order oot means. Y' put doon aall the things y' MIGHT need, an' y' forget aall the things yore SARTIN t' need. An' b' Thorsda', oot o' yor order, y've got almond essence, cocoa, vinegar, fruit-salts, fire-lighters, starch, coffee, an' a tin o' mustard y' hevn't needed an' nowt t' myek a puddin' with, an' nee money t' buy owt for the dinnor, cass yor grosseries left y' skint.

Porsnal shoppin', buyin' watt y' want when y' want it is the best. But even theor thor's a snag.

Y' gan intiv a shop, intendin' t' buy a tin o' floor polish, an' a delicious smell meets y' as y' step inside. The customer afore ye's been buyin' some cyukked ham. An' sitch ham! Theor it is – lean, an' pink, an' form [firm]. Y' cannit afford it, cass it wud tyek at least half a pund t' give each o' ye's a slice, an' five-bob jist for a tea-time treat wud be sinful extravagance.

"A tin o' floor-polish," y' say formly. An' then – aal biv itsel' yor tongue says, "And half a pund o' cyukked ham." An' then when teatime comes y' cannit injoy yor ham for wonderin' watt the fambly 'll say the morra' when the' find the dinner is pan-hagglety myed wi' tyetties, a onion, an' a bit bacon skin t' giv it a bit tyest. An' even the smell o' yor fresh-polished floor bothers y' cass it reminds y' hoo y've spent six bob instead of o' one-an'-tuppence.

Thor's ondly one kind o' shoppin' that['s] aal sheer injoyment, an' that's when y' hev – say, a pund – that's aall yor aan, an' that y' kin squaander onny way y' like. It's a thing that disn't happen varry often. But when it diz happen, it's a experience wawth hevvin'.

Even the gettin' riddy t' gan out is excitin'. Thor's a feelin' in the air like Bank Hallida', an' yor aad tweed coat an' yor broon snood hat jist wain't dee. Y' feel like a millionaire, an' fre the skin oot, yo're dressed in yor best.

Till y' get amang the shop[s] y' hevn't reelised wat a selection o' ticin' things kin be bowt for a pund. Shud y' buy a few luxurious bits o' nic-naffs y've aalwiz wanted? For yor pund y' cud buy a lace-edged hanky, and a chiffon scarf, and a sequined evenin' bag. Or y' cud buy some gud perfume. Or some nice gloves.

Maist likely y'll end up buyin' vests for the bairns. But it wuz a nice aftornyun aall the syem, an' a lump different t' yor usual shoppin'.

Teapots

Standin' on the front-room trolley,
In the maist conspicuous place
Is a handsome silver teapot.
Aa wud coont it a disgrace
If it wazn't polished daily.
An' Aa'm sure ye'd nivvor guess,
When yo' saa me handsome teapot,
That it's jist "E.P.N.S."
But jist luk aroond the kitchen.
What's that stannin' on the hob?
It's a fat broon <u>boody</u> teapot,   earthenware
An' it's aalwis on the job.
If Aa'm feelin' tired an' weory
Throbbin' heid, an' swollen feet
Then the canny aad broon teapot
Myeks a brew thut puts its reet.

An' mee friends is like me teapots.
Some is shams, jist for display.
At the forst faint sign o' trouble
Aih – Hoo sharp the' haadaway!
But thor's other's vastly different.
"Aad-brood-teapot-friends," in fact.
When Aa'm needin' help, or comfort
By! Hoo quickly the' kin act!

Aye. Thor's some that's plain broon <u>bood</u>,   body
An' thor's some "E.P.N.S."
Some is friends in time o' trouble
Some keeps friendship for success.

Bairns' Bullets [children's sweets]

This week, Aa've got another grouse.

The fact is, folks, wor bairns is bein' chet [cheated] o' one o' life's greatest joys, an' Aa kin see nee need fo'd [for it].

In waartime, it wuz different. Sweets wuz rationed, an' the "points" wuz a clart [nuisance], an' it wuz natchril that w' shad save time an' trouble b' buyin' wor week's supply all at once, in quaarters or halfpunds.

But the waar's been ower for ten veers; an' thor's nee reason at call wy bairns shudn't be yebble [able] t' spend thor pocket-money in a bairnish way; or wy bairnish bullets [sweets] shudn't be manufactured like the' used t' be.

When Aa tell wor bairns aboot the things Aa cud buy wi' me Serrida's penny, it seems like a fairy tale. Aa describe a bar o' "Yankee-Panky" – Pink an' white taffy, it wuz wiv a bull-roarer lapped up wiv it. Noo watt bairn's gaan t' prefer a quaarter o' caramels t' that?

Thor wuz Lucky Tyetties, Lucky Horseshoes, an' Ring Candy. The tyetties an' horseshoes had little silvery charms in them, an ivry stick o' Ring Candy had a joowelled ring aroond it.

Aa knaa y' cannit expect t' buy owt like this for a hap'ny nooadays; but that's nee reason wy the' shudn't be theor for bairns t' buy. The' hev the pocket-money t' match the times; an' the' hev t' buy rowlls o' winegums, poor bairns! Bullets isn't interestin' like the' used t' be.

"Pit Props" wuz thick logs o' coconutty candy; an' fine shreddy coconut covered wi' choclit pooda' wuz "Bacey." "Bull's Eyes" changed colour as y' sucked them – an' a bullet lasts a lot langer if y' keep tyekkin' it oot o' yor mooth t' see watt colour it is noo.

"Seaside Mixture" luked like real shells an' pebbles: an' y' cud buy little "sacks" o' tyetties or peas or oranges. Thor wuz barley-sugar not in stright sober sticks like noo, but in coarse shiney nobbles, clagged roond a bit twine. Thor wuz crystal clear fishes – reed an' yella an' white; thor wuz Summer Snow – a sort o' flavoured sugary pooda' that y' et b' suckin' yor finger an' dabbin' it in the pooda' an' suckin' it off. It lasted a lung time!

Wi' sharbet, y' had a interestin choice. Thor wuz Sharbet Dabs, wheor y' got a dab o' taffy on a stick, watt y' licked and dabbed in yor sharbet, and thor wuz Sharbet Foontins, wheor y' sucked the sharbet up through a chube o' lickrish.

Thor wuz Nigger Babies, Lickrish Telephones, Lickrish Byut-laces, Lickrish Blaa-Baals, Lickrish Pipes. W' had nivvor hord o' Child Psychology in them days but manufacturers knew watt appealed t' bairns.

It's not intirely extinct, thank gudness. Sometimes y' kin come across a little shop w' the reet things t' sell – an' the reet porson t' sell them.

Yistida' Aa watched wor Petal spend tuppence.

Sh' bowt a hap'orth o' Spearmint Bouncers, a hap'orth o Firebaalls, a hap'orth o' Aniseed Baalls, an' a Gob-Stopper. Y' cannit weigh a proportion o' bullets that's sivinpence a quaarter, so the forst three "shares" had t' be coonted; an' the wife went t' fower seprit jars t' serve the bairn an' orn the profit off tuppence. Theor wuz patience.

Mevvies it's not bairns' bullets that's scarce, but understandin' hearts, an' kindliness, an' gud nature – the sort o' thing y' get in little corner shops wheor the wife ahint the coonter is the bairns' friend, an' not jist a cog in the wheel o' Big Business.

Ideal Homes

Ivry noo an' then, at exhibitions or in the pages o' glossy magazines w' see demonstations an' pickshers o' watt's supposed t' be "Ideal Homes." The queeor thing is that though these hyems is porfect, w' nivvor feel w' want t' swap them for wor aan hyems. Heor an' theor thor'll be bits w' wud like to hev, or copy. But Aa wud like t' bet that if onny wife wuz invited t' exchange 'or hyem, – leavin' ivrythink ahint – for one o' these porfect hyems, she wud torn the offer doon.

For one thing, the porfect hoose didn't cater for sentiment.

In varny ivry hoose, thor's summack w' grew up with, for instance. In wor hoose, the "summack" is a little cracket. The legs is ridged b' generations o' cats' claas. Thor's a smaall roond hole in the middle that wuz myed t' howld the wull-winder me Da invented. Aa used t' stand on that cracket t' luk oot the winda'; spread me hanky on it an' arrange me tin tea-set for a dolls' party; or torn it upside doon an' shove it roond for a pram. An' on Serrida' neet eftor Aa had been bathed Aa wud be allowed t' sit on the cracket in me neetgoon an' read me that week's Penny Popular Classic – "Her Benny," "Jessica's First Prayer" or summack, while me hair dried.

Noo in a porfect hoose thor wud be nee place for a cracket like that. Mevvies in the scullery – if Aa enamelled the legs an' formica'd the top. But then it wadn't be maa cracket. It wud jist be "a stool."

An' oh – them stream-lined clinic-lukkin' Kitchens! Watt wife in 'or reet senses wants t' scuttle roond within a little square composed o' fridge, sink, drainin'-board, wesher, table, cooker, cab'nit, an' "preparation area?" Wheor, in a kitchen like that, cud the cat get kittens, or the dog gnaa 'ees bones? Or the bairns stand thor jar o' frog-spawn? Aa defy onnybody in a kitchen like that t' sit in a rockin'-chair while tho're waitin' o' summack broonin', or comin' t' the boil; or start trimmin' a hat, say, while the breid's risin'…

16. 'Memories of the Coal Fired Kitchen Range' (1930s) by Joyce Oxley

The kitchen range, or 'the fireplace' as it was usually called was the heart of the house. It was the first place you looked at coming downstairs in the morning and coming from school on the cold dark winter afternoons. Each morning my Mother would give it a little poke and shake, and when the coals 'brightened' up would get the blazer and it wasn't long before we had a good fire burning, ready for a good rake-out and then the coals lying on the back of the fire hole all night would be pulled down and it was away for another day! The first time I saw the fire out and the clean empty grate was the morning we left that house – I was 9 years old. It looked so strange, I've never forgotten it.

The fireplace took up most of one wall – back-to-back with the one next door. There was a cupboard at one side which was always warm and dry. Things like salt and sugar were kept there, along with the dish of butter in use, and it was always stacked out with cups and saucers and all sorts of china and dishes. Next to this was the big, round oven with a drop-down door and a polished brass handle. It was a great treat if you had your supper on the open door with your feet on the fender. This only happened if you had a cold, weren't very well (or 'weren't varry clivver' as we used to say). The inside of the oven was whitewashed and had two heavy metal shelves. These were taken out and wrapped in a bit of blanket and used to warm the beds. The heat was controlled by dampers which I knew nothing about, and all the bread, cakes, and tarts were baked in that oven. I still don't know how our Mothers knew the correct temperature just by rolling up their sleeve and testing the heat on their bare arm…

The dinner was cooked on the open fire. The front bar (where the kettle usually stood) could be turned right over on to the fire, and the long poker and fire tongs would be laid behind it. You could balance three or four pans on this. Usually the big pan with the suet pudding wrapped in a cloth went on first, as it took ages for a good pudding. Then a steamer full of potatoes was fitted on top, and a lid covered the lot. Smaller pans for vegetables cooked on the turned-over bar and away they went. The frying pan went on the bar, and the chip pan also as it was a firmer base. I don't remember any accidents wth the fire apart from the kettle boiling over and scattering ashes and water and making an awful smell and we would say 'the kettle's cowped!' I was only warned to keep back when the chip pan was on the fire, and at jam and jelly making time. My Mam had a name for making blackberry jelly and chutneys. It must have been an awful job standing over the fire stirring a steaming pan. Sometimes her face was nearly the colour of the jelly with the heat!

The set pot was on the other side of the fire. The water in there was always hot enough for most jobs and it could be made to boil when needed for sheets and towels. It was filled by hand – pails of cold water poured in the top and a flat lid fitted on. This was our only source of hot water. Some had a little brass top on the front to empty it, but I don't think ours had as I can remember, it being emptied with the 'tin pot' into a pail. This was a straight sided enamel pot with a big handle on the side – about a quart. We called it the tin pot, others called it the laden- or lathen-pot. The sheets and towels were lifted out with the help of the 'poss stick' – a sturdy stick about 2 feet long used for lifting the clothes out of the hot water. Usually a neighbour helped with this as it was a heavy job heaving them out of the boiler and into the tin bath waiting in the fireplace. They were carried outside and left to cool off before going through the mangle – washing was a tough job in those days!

The fire was never allowed to go out. It was raked clean at bedtime, a shovel of coal put on and then damped down with small coal and coal duff which kept it smouldering all night. A couple of buckets of coal were thrown onto the back of the fire where there was a sort of ledge and these were ready to be pulled down on to the fire when needed with the colrake (coal rake). I can still hear the 'wumph' as the people next door 'hoyed' their coal on the fireback before they went to bed.

On New Year's Eve the fire was thoroughly cleaned out and a new fire started from the little bit left in the grate. The hearth was washed and tidied up ready for the First Foot who brought in the New Year. He always had a lump of coal for luck. My husband always brought in coal and a small log or a bundle of sticks and walked over to the fire and put them on top of last year's fire.

The whole fireplace was kept bright and shining – it was a point of honour. A kind of blacklead you moistened (usually with spit) in a tin with a picture of a zebra on the lid was used – I think it was called Ze-bo. It was brushed on and then polished hard till it gleamed. Even the space under the fire was whitewashed on a Friday. I used to like to hear it sizzle when it was brushed on to the hot bricks. We had a tidy which fitted round the front of the fire to stop the ashes from getting on to the hearth, and a steel fender, shining like silver, just the right height to sit on, but if you sat on the bit in front of the fire it was too hot for comfort! The hearth itself was whitewashed. Later, you could buy a sheet of thin zinc with a pattern on – I think it was called a hearth plate – which fitted over the hearth. This was very popular as it only needed to be washed over.

There was a polished brass rail running the length of the fireplace, used to warm clothes, and a wooden mantlepiece which had a nice coloured strip of cloth tacked to it – I think it was a called a mantle cloth. On the mantlepiece stood a nice old clock in a short case belonging to my Grandad who always wound it up himself. He always checked it with his pocket watch and said 'Aye, man' but whether that meant it was fast or slow I never found out. All the gun and dog licences and other important papers were stuffed behind it. There was a pair of brass candlesticks and two white china dogs with gold chains round their necks. We called them Vic and Bess after our two springer spaniels; and there was a spike for the store checks along with several pipes and matchboxes and Mam's purse and other bits and pieces. If anyone mislaid anything you always looked on the mantlepiece first – it was nearly always there.

Yes, the fireplace was truly the most important part of the home.

17. 'A Royal Feast' from Scott Dobson, 'Stotty Cake Row', (1971)

Noo ah'm gan [I'm going] te tell ye somethin' – but keep it te yorsel or we'll aall get fetched up b' the poliss. We had a swan for wor Christmas dinner. Aye – a swan. Ye divvent hev te tell us — aah knaa.

It's a royal bord an' yer not supposed te shut [shoot] swans – but wor Fred shut this one be accident. Mind ah towld him off.

"That's the Queens' prerogative ye fond gonniel [fool]" ah towld him. "We'll be heyvin' the Hoosehold Cavalry doon heor if she gets te knaa – how would ye like it if she myed off with that aad clocker [hen] o' yours oot o' the henhoose?"

But it wes ower late te de owt aboot it – but ah'll nivor forget the night he done it. He'd been oot shuttin' aall day an' ah heors his motor-bike an' side-car stop ootside wor hoose aboot midnight.

"Anybody aboot?" he sez – stickin' his heed [head] roond the door and lukkin' deed guilty. Whey ah went oot te give him a hand – when ah saa the size o' the body in the sidecar ah thowt he'd done a morder.

By – what a gigantic bord – it lukked as big as the flamin' Concorde. "Ah died a thoosand deaths cummin' doon that North Road" sez Fred. "Ivvory time ah seed a car with a leet on top ah thowt it was the poliss – thor wor nowt but taxis though."

Whey we had te git rid o' the evidence afore mornin' so we sets to. We wor up till the crack o' dawn ploatin' [plucking] and cleanin' that bord – ah missed a shift.

When wor lass gets up she teks one luk. "Ye'll nivvor get that in wor oven", she sez. Mind she wez reet an aall. We had te saa [saw] it in two.

B' then the nyebours is up and what wi' wor backyard bein' full o' feathers we had te slip them half of it te keep thor mooths shut.

Then we had te stuff it afore we cooked it. Mistress Barker at the corner shop gives us an aad-fashioned look when ah buys up all hor stock o' sage and onions.

"What on orth hey ye got for yor Christmas dinner", she sez. "A gowlden eagle?"

Mind – its been champion, luvly rich meat but wor aall sick of it. Ah knaa what me bait's gan te be [food's going to be] for the next fortneet. Swan sandwiches, curried swan, potted swan, swan rissoles — ye name them ah'll be gettin' thim.

But mind what ah telt ye – not a word or we'll aall be fetched up – an aa've got ne desire te spend New Year in the Toor o' London.

18. 'Adam and Eve and the Apple', from John Green's 'Tales and Ballads of Wearside' (1871)

Hendy is explaining a picture of the Garden of Eden to his marra Geodie (Geordie)…

"Now then," said Hendy, resuming his story, "Adam and Eve was put into a fine gawden [garden] – a grit big un – mevies as lang as frev [from] here ti Ryhope; Nobel's gawdens wad n't gie tha onny idear on't – nut a bit. Now thou sees, Geodie, they had a purfit reet tiv onnythink i' that gawden: grosers [gooseberries], rubab, cherries, pears, curnberries [currants], tumaters, taties [potatoes], turmots [turnips], cabbish, an' brockley; aye, an' even the varry sour dockens [sorrel] eff they liked. But there was one big apple tree, Geodie, that was growin' reet i' the middle o' that gawden, an' they hadn't ti eat o' the fruit o' that tree upon nee account whatsomiver.

Now it happened one moanin' just efther Adam had getten his brikwast, he put on this hat, an' he ses tiv his wife: 'Eve,' he says, 'aw'se just gawn [going] as far as the summer-hoose ti smoke my pipe, an' when thoo gans out for ti get the vigitables for the broth, mind thou keeps off that apple tree.' Now Geodie, thou's a married man, an' aw'se [I'm] a married man, an' thou knaws, an' aw knaw, that eff ye keep harp, harpin' on day efther day tiv a woman nut for ti gan an' dee [do] a thing, it's just the varry way for ti mack her gan an di'd [do it].

Just about ten minnits efther he'd gyen out, she pops out an' all, wiv a bit basket ti put the greens in, swingin' iv her hand, an' a grit big straw hat on her heed ti keep the sun off her fyece. Away she gans steppin' out like a three-year-awd, past all the carrots, turmots, an' cabbish, an' niver stops till she gets slap underneath that varry apple tree. She tuck a good luck, an' man, the apples did luck [look] bonny, she cudn't stand the temptashon nee langer, so she clicks up a styen [snatches up a stone], an' let drive amang the brenches, an' down comes a big rusty coat [red-skinned apple]; an' it wasn't lang afore her teeth was intid [into it]. She knock'd down another one, an' put it intiv her pocket, an' when Adam cam' hyem, she tell'd him what she'd deun, an' pursuaded the poor daft man ti eat the tother one; an' next moanin' they were byeth [both] o' them turn'd out."

"Wy man," Geodie exclaimed when Hendy had finished his narrative. "Aw dinnot knaw see [so] much about his bein' daft; lucks tha Hendy, eff aw'd had a wife as bonny as that woman i' the pickter, an' she'd axed us, aw wad hev gyen inti the law [low] street, down the dark entry, an' eaten all the apples out ov a Frenchman's howld."